Be An
Outrageous Older Woman
A RASP*

* Remarkable Aging Smart Person

Also by Ruth Harriet Jacobs, Ph.D.

Life After Youth: Female, Forty — What Next?

Button, Button, Who Has the Button?

Re-Engagement in Later Life: Re-Employment and Remarriage
with Barbara H. Vinick

Older Women Surviving and Thriving: A Manual

We Speak For Peace

Out of Their Mouths

Be An Outrageous Older Woman
A RASP

Ruth Harriet Jacobs, Ph.D.

KNOWLEDGE, IDEAS & TRENDS
Publisher
MANCHESTER, CONNECTICUT

Cover design: Bob Josen
Text design: Leslie Sanborn

First published in 1993 by:
Knowledge, Ideas & Trends, Inc.
1131-0 Tolland Turnpike, Suite 175
Manchester, CT 06040
(800) 826-0529

Publication Data

Jacobs, Ruth Harriet
    Be an outrageous older woman: A RASP: remarkable aging smart person / Ruth Harriet Jacobs

    Includes bibliographical references.
    ISBN 1-879198-23-1
    1. Aged women—United States. 2. Self-help techniques. 3. Life skills. I. Title.
    HQ1064.V5 J322
    305.4 - dc20

10 9 8 7 6 5 4 3 2

Revised edition
Printed in the United States of America

Contents

CHAPTER

ONE Don't Rage; Be Outrageous 1

TWO Trouble Making 9

THREE Real Life Outrageousness 17

FOUR Changing Identity 25

FIVE New Selves 39

SIX How to Select Helpers 49

SEVEN Being Creative 69

EIGHT House Yourself Creatively 81

NINE Units of Belongingness 95

TEN Be Outrageous with Your Descendants 101

ELEVEN Sexuality 117

TWELVE Being Politically Outrageous 137

THIRTEEN Having Fun 147

FOURTEEN Prime Time Women's Friendship 153

FIFTEEN Handling Outrageous Incidents 163

SIXTEEN Bereavement: Hurting and Healing 171

SEVENTEEN Paid Work 179

EIGHTEEN Alphabet for Economizing 189

NINETEEN Benefits of Aging 197

TWENTY Graduation and Commencement 203

TWENTY-ONE Post Graduation 207

Index 237

Acknowledgments

The author would like to thank Sandra Brown and Rita McCullough, President and Vice President of KIT, for their faith in this book and for having the courage to start a press in difficult times. She thanks the International Women's Writing Guild for making it possible for her to meet Rita McCullough at its 1990 Conference at Skidmore College.

She would like to thank her daughter, Edith Jane Jacobs, and son, Eliha Jacobe, for their encouragement and also Ruth Murphy, M.D., and Theodore Spielberg, M.D.

She is grateful to the Stone Center at Wellesley College for its funding for her work on depression in older women and to the National Institute of Mental Health, the National Science Foundation, and the United States Department of Education for funding. She is especially grateful to the Wellesley College Center for Research on Women for its support and inspiration.

She would also like to thank the many women, friends, interviewees, workshop participants, and others whose ideas and experiences are reflected in this book.

CHAPTER ONE

Don't Rage; Be Outrageous

RAGE is in the middle of the word outrage-ous. Rage occurs when we are frustrated, ignored, hurt, trivialized, denied needed resources, insulted, treated as second class individuals, and in other ways injured. In our society, women are often discrimi-nated against when they age. This can be as major and open as not being hired or as subtle as being treated as though we are invisible or as being treated perfunctorily at social gatherings. When we brood about this and take no action, our rage or anger often goes inward, turn-ing into depression or passivity.

However, we can move beyond rage by being OUT RAGE OUS older women, refusing to accept the stereotypes or slights. This book will give you recipes for coming out of rage and into being a magnifi-cent older woman who takes what she can from life to be happy, to be productive, and, above all, to laugh. We need joy in our lives as we age. There are decrements in aging, but we can be creative about increments.

At 70, I have learned that if you are outrageous enough, good things happen. You stop being invisible and become validated. For example, in 1987, I decided to call myself a R.A.S.P. I had never been a W.A.S.P. (White Anglo Saxon Protestant) because, among other dis-qualifications, I am the wrong ethnic group and too fat. But I figured I could RASP my way though my older years fighting for my own rights and my own joy and for those of other older women. To me, R.A.S.P. stood for Remarkable Aging Smart Person, and I painted it on a T Shirt *and* Sweat Shirt to handle all seasons. I also made a R.A.S.P. button by putting masking tape over the button of a disliked

1

politician and writing R.A.S.P. with a magic marker, bright red, of course.

Other women suggested R.A.S.P. also stood for, as the situation warranted, Ravishing Aging Sexy Person or Radical Aging Strategic Person. Wherever I went, I invited mature women to join R.A.S.P., explaining that it was a great organization because there were no dues, meetings, newsletter, or financial appeals. Other R.A.S.P. buttons began to appear. By 1990, the prestigeful American Aging Society sent me an unsolicited letter addressed to Ruth Jacobs, President of R.A.S.P., inviting me and my members to join. If the American Aging Society says R.A.S.P. is real, it must be. It's no longer just my private joke. So now I ask you to join R.A.S.P.

In this book, you will learn how to start Rasping. What I will offer comes from more than my personal experience. It comes from the research, teaching, and advocacy on women and aging that I have done since I earned my Ph. D., in sociology in 1969, at age 45 (after getting my B.S. at age 40 while my children were in school). I am the older women's Dr. Ruth, come to tell the truth, and I hope by the time I'm done, you'll think I am the better one.

My research and my work on behalf of older women has been supported by such agencies as the National Institute of Mental Health, the National Science Foundation, the U.S. Department of Education, the Stone Center for Women's Development and Services at Wellesley College, and the Wellesley College Center for Research on Women where I have been affiliated since the seventies. I have learned a great deal from wonderful aging women who have taken my "Older Women Surviving and Thriving Workshops" and from women I have interviewed for my research books and articles. Many of them, like me, had to overcome the internalized cultural bias against aging, especially against aging women.

My own crisis of aging came when I was sixty, an age that signaled to me the end of mid-life. When I was nearly 61, I wrote in a poem how I had conquered my fears.

Becoming Sixty

There were terror and anger
at coming into sixty.
Would I give birth
only to my old age?

Now near sixty-one
I count the gifts
that sixty gave.

A book flowed from my life
to those who needed it
and love flowed back to me.

In a yard that had seemed full,
space for another garden appeared.
I took my aloneness to Quaker meeting,
and my outstretched palms were filled.

I walked further along the beach,
swam longer in more sacred places,
danced the spiral dance,
reclaimed daisies for women
in my ritual for a precious friend
and received poet's wine
from a new friend who came
in the evening of my need.

In addition to the things listed in the poem, I tried many other new activities the year I became sixty. By 63, I was really enjoying my older womanhood and asking myself what I wanted to do with the rest of my life.

Please write down now what you want to do with the rest of your life.

When I did my list, I discovered I no longer wanted to work full time teaching and chairing the sociology department at Clark University, and I resigned to teach only part time elsewhere and to do other things. Writing the list made me confront my life and change it. It is easy to stick to a known old safe-but-uncomfortable identity. We have to shake ourselves up once in a while. Writing to ourselves can give us access to our deep wishes as my poem which follows did for me.

At Sixty-three

What I want for the rest of my life
is to live simply and joyfully
close to nature and God
ministering, as I am led to do
to people in new ways,
communicating with my children
as equals without dependency
or guilt on either side
or the reliving of old history.

What I want for the rest of my life
is to accept that in my living
I made serious mistakes
but did the best I could at the time.
I want to stop blaming myself
and have as much compassion and respect
for myself as I have for others.

I want to travel to new places
to witness and be touched
by the stories of others
then tell their stories
in my books and poetry
to help people see themselves
in others and know we are all
kindred spirits within the spirit,
and that what injures one of us

insults all of us
while the triumph of one of us
is a mountain climbed by all.

What I want for the rest of my life
is to deal gracefully and graciously
with the decrements of aging
so that by example and testimony
I give others the courage
to see that the missions and ministry
of the aged are as important as of youth
and are important to youth.

Finally, I want to meet my death knowing
that I lived fully, returning to life
the talents and time given me by grace.

Friendly Woman Vol. 8, No. 7

Aging gives us a chance to know ourselves and to learn the meaning of life. Also, I have learned, as you should, to enjoy the perks of being older. When a passenger, I happily accept the front seat in two door cars that require pretzel crawling to get to the back, I am delighted when the 16 year old movie cashiers ask, "Senior citizen ticket?" which is half price. I graciously accept snow shoveling help, but I will not tolerate being considered mentally incompetent. In response to the people who try to curry favor in a youth oriented society by calling me and other older women "young woman," I say:

Don't call me a young woman;
it's not a compliment or courtesy
but rather a grating discourtesy.
Being old is a hard won achievement
not something to be brushed aside
treated as infirmity or ugliness
or apologized away by "young woman."
I am an old woman, a long liver.
I'm proud of it. I revel in it.
I wear my grey hair and wrinkles
as badges of triumphant survival
and I intend to grow even older.

Don't call me a young woman.
I was a young woman for years
but that was then and this is now.
I was a mid life woman for a time
and I celebrated that good span.
Now I am somebody magnificent, new,
a seer, wise woman, old proud crone,
an example and mentor to the young
who need to learn old women wisdom.
I look back on jobs well done
and learn to do different tasks now.
I think great thoughts and share them.

Don't call me a young woman.
You reveal your own fears of aging.
Maybe you'd better come learn from
all of us wonderful old women
how to take the sum of your life
with all its experience and knowledge
and show how a fully developed life
can know the joy of a past well done
and the joy of life left to live.

Sadly, some women deny their aging, lie about their age to themselves and others, and like being called "young woman." This is not
surprising in view of the ageism in society which we internalize. Many
of us do not have good models of women who aged well, who were
magnificent and outrageous. Often women reject women older than
themselves or even women their own age, saying they prefer younger
women. They are really rejecting themselves as they age. I hope to help
you come to terms with this.

When we were children, we learned how to act from stories; we
learned what we could be like when we were older. We also had real
life models in older siblings, parents, neighbors, heroes, and heroines.
As older women, we need models of how to live our lives courageously
and humorously, and I think stories can help us with this. Unfortunately, there are too few of them. In the next chapter, I present a piece

of my fiction in which an older woman took the lead in advocacy for older people and had fun in the process. It appeared in *Broomstick*,* a magazine by and for women over forty published by two outrageous older California women.

---

* *Broomstick: Options for Women Over Forty*, 3543 18th Street, #3, San Francisco, CA 94110.

CHAPTER TWO

Trouble Making

MY TROUBLE-MAKING started because I was on a television program arranged by the college where I have been taking courses since I retired five years ago. At 65, I stopped teaching fourth grade and started living for me, Bessie. A couple of other folks and I were to talk about going to school after retirement. Instead, I decided to inform the audience about the problems many old people have these days. I said that the housing situation was terrible for low-income persons of all ages but especially hard on the old. I got carried away and said it was time to start an organization of troublemakers. I looked right at the camera and invited interested folks to meet at 10 A.M. the next day in the student lounge at the college.

Seventy-three women and nine men showed up, mostly old people, but eighteen young college students also came. Everyone introduced herself or himself and then said what her or his problem was. One woman said, "I have to share a bedroom with four grandchildren." Some had been thrown out of their apartments that were being converted to condos they couldn't afford. Others would like to get out of places that were decrepit, cold, unsanitary, and unsafe. Why, there were even homeless folks who were living in shelters, terrible temporary arrangements, or even in their cars or on the streets. A nursing home resident said she had to enter the institution because she couldn't find affordable housing. A 75 year old man from a building that had been condemned and razed admitted that he lived at the college, spending days in the student lounge and nights in the library which is open 24 hours a day. He said, "It's not so bad; the students sneak me into the gym for showers and bring me doggie bags from the cafeteria."

Mary reported she has been living in a place without heat for two years and laughs when she reads about the danger to old people of hypothermia. "I can't do anything *but* laugh," she said, nearly crying. Emily, who moved into her daughter's when her house went condo, is afraid her son-in-law is out of patience and taking it out on his wife.

David, the man living at the college, said, "In my opinion, instead of putting up that new state office building which is opening next week, they should have put up low-income housing for us." Then, a woman with a gray bun and frilly clothes looked up from her knitting and said, "Why don't we take over that building for old folks that don't have any homes?" Everyone in the room clapped.

Emily said, "Oh, they won't let us stay. We're just a bunch of old people."

Rosalind, who had made the suggestions, said, "Maybe. But at least we will call attention to our plight. Nothing has worked up until now." A man, Ralph, added, "Well, at least we will have some fun. I have been so bored since they forced me to retire last year."

Then we all held hands and pledged that everyone would keep our plan a secret. After that, we set up task forces to get stuff we would need. The students volunteered to transport us, and Emily said her son-in-law, who would do anything to get rid of her, would donate the use of his truck to bring in mattresses and other supplies.

Nora announced, "I'll make a flag with a house appliqued on it."

Charles said, "Don't worry about how to get into the building. I used to be a custodian at the State House before they forced me to retire. I get so lonely, I go down to visit the guys all the time. Some of them have been transferred to the new building. I've seen the master keys hanging in the basement. I'll go in tomorrow, hide in the basement, and let you all in during the dead of night."

"Isn't there a night watchman?" Rosalind asked.

"No, they overspent on buying materials from the Governor's cronies, and ran out of funds for a night custodian," Charles said.

Charles did what he said. He did even more. The new cafeteria had been stocked well, and he had coffee waiting for us along with the cookies that were to be for the opening reception. It is a good thing he made plenty of coffee because people from our meeting had brought their friends. Rosalind and I counted 118 people, a bowl of goldfish, 32 dogs, and 17 cats. Twelve of the college students who had driven us insisted on staying in the building with us. Four admitted that they wanted to avoid exams, and three explained that they were going to write papers about us. We figured the other five were committed to our cause or just wanted an experience. We figured they would have one.

Everyone had brought food, but the cafeteria was so well stocked in anticipation of the building opening, that it was unnecessary. Two tall students hung our flag on the plaza and put up signs on the glass doors saying "Old Age Housing." The other students helped Charles use the lumber in the basement to nail shut all the other entrances to the building. We barricaded the front doors with mattresses on the floors and assigned people shifts to lie on those mattresses. The folks who were not on the first shift to barricade roamed the building, finding offices which they could establish as their homes. There were more offices than we needed so folks took the best ones. Of course, the ones with nice windows were for the elected and appointed state officials; the secretaries were to get the ones without windows.

Everyone insisted that I take the Governor's office for my home. I felt piggish because it was great so I invited Rosalind and Emily to share it. The carpet was so thick we hardly needed mattresses at all, and the bar was already stocked so we figured we should give some parties there for the rest of the gang. There was a nice little refrigerator loaded with cheese and expensive olives. As I was admiring the Governor's office, Ralph came up to get me. There was a reporter at the door who wanted to come in. One of the students, a journalism major, had called him about our operation. "Sure, let him come in," I said. "Let's put him in the state public relations office, and he can call our story out to his paper."

Our reporter, Bob, had brought a photographer who took lots of pictures of us, and then we let him out of the building. Bob stayed in. He was very excited. "I haven't covered a good sit-in since the seventies," he said.

Then we made a directory of who was in what office and what the phone numbers at these new "homes" were. People called their families.

In the morning, as people were just starting to walk on the streets around the building, some of them came up to the building to look in at us and hold up headlines on their newspapers. These headlines said, "Senior Citizens Occupy New State Office Building." Soon, the phones in the building began to ring and we answered them. A lot of the calls were from newspapers and radio stations and television reporters wanting to interview us and get an update on the story they had copied from Bob's newspaper. Other reporters came to the door, and we handed out some press releases our retired secretaries had typed and xeroxed on the new machines in the building.

We hung a clothesline in the lobby, and our people hung their most photogenic clothes on it for the photographers who took pictures through the glass doors.

The Governor himself came to the door at noon, and we opened it a crack. He shouted through it, "This is ridiculous. I want you out of this building in a hour."

We chanted, "No, no, no, we won't go, we dare, we care about old age housing. We have to stay here because there isn't enough low cost housing, and rents are high as the sky."

After the Governor left, we heard on the radio that the Governor had decided to do nothing because he figured that we would get sick of the stunt in a day or two and leave.

He said, "I don't want to call out the State Police against a bunch of helpless, harmless old nuts, I mean people." The commentators said that the Governor was afraid of losing the old age vote if he did anything.

Pretty soon lots of people came by the building bringing us things. We would open the doors a smidgen and accept food, blankets, clothes, wine, radios, games. A women's organization sent us a huge bunch of roses. A restaurant donated huge buckets of chicken, and a fast food chain sent so many hamburgers that we had enough for all the dogs and cats because we had too much food. Linda became our chief cook. She was ecstatic. "I used to cook for my family, but lately I have been living in a room with only a hot plate. What a joy to have this great cafeteria kitchen and all the staples and frozen stuff that were put in for the opening."

When we needed anything, we mentioned it to Bob, our reporter, or the reporters who called. We got a little cynical because firms would call the radio station announcing what they were donating.

A couple of our folks had forgotten their medications, but our retired physician called their drugstores and got the medicines delivered fast. Some folks said the street lights kept them awake the first night so we asked the reporters to announce that we needed some curtains, and they were donated by two companies. Local college students chipped in and bought us stereos and records and a television to amuse us. But they under-estimated us. By the third day, we had little free time because we organized adult education courses on current events, ancient history, tenants' rights, poetry, novels, creative aging and ageism, public relations techniques, and lots of other things. We had exercise groups, dance groups, drawing groups, consciousness raising groups, and lots more. Our education committee operated out of the state department of education office. We used the long corridors for walks.

Every day at 10, we had a community meeting for everyone. We held it in the front lobby so the reporters could see it, and the students rigged up a loud speaker system so folks on the plaza could hear it. All the equipment came from the state's public relations office in the building.

As the days passed, more and more people came to the plaza to peer in at us. A man set up a booth outside the building to sell Elder Power buttons. Another man sold "Elderburgers." A third entrepreneur had replicas of our house flag made in Korea and flown in to sell at $5 each.

The reporters interviewed people on the street about us. One man offered to donate his mother-in-law to our effort and another his wife. We didn't like these "jokes" that put down women. Such sexist jibes are not funny.

Each day, the Governor came to the building and asked us to leave, and we explained we couldn't until housing was available elsewhere for those in the state who needed it. The Governor asked if we would leave if he set up an emergency task force, on housing. David said, "Set up the task force and we'll see what it does."

Lots of old folks and many young ones arrived asking to join us. We decided to let each tell her or his story over the loudspeakers for the press and to admit those who were most needy. We admitted a woman who had been living in a train station for eight months, a man who had been living in his car until it was stolen, a person who had escaped a nursing home, and others. One day, the Governor's mother arrived and said she was sick of living with her son and daughter-in-law. We admitted her.

Just after that, on the tenth day, the Governor said he would shut off our telephones and electricity if we did not get out. Editorials appeared saying, "What will happen if elders fall and break bones?" and "Sick elders will be unable to get help." The radio announced that thousands of people called the Governor's office protesting the Governor waging war against the old.

Just in case he did it, college students organized a candle drive, and students all the way from nursery schools to colleges formed a human chain passing what seemed a million candles through our crack. People watching danced around the hugh pile of candles in the plaza and cheered.

At our community meeting, we voted to stay even if the power went off, and we heard that lots of folks pledged to keep us supplied with whatever we needed. Rosalind asked for yarn, and so much arrived we donated it to the Red Cross.

At this point, we had been in the building two weeks, long enough, in fact, for some nice little romances to begin and become consummated among us. Rosalind and Emily had moved out of my quarters because I was sharing with a nice man who had joined us.

The Governor begged for a sit down meeting with us instead of a conversation through the crack. We agreed, let him in the building, and ushered him into what was to have been his office. He blanched when he saw the red chintz curtains I had put up and the nice little dust ruffle I had put around his desk. He wanted to know what arrangements we had for the dogs, and I assured him that we kept paper and plastic on the floors in the cellar where we walked them. I apologized because we had eaten his cheese, but I did offer him a little cup of chicken soup from the pot simmering on the hot plate on his desk.

"Let's be reasonable," he said. "You can't stay here forever."

Rosalind replied, "Many of us have lived in worse places." Then the Governor stated, "It's illegal."

"It is immoral not to take care of Americans who need housing," Rosalind said.

The Governor looked like he was going to cry. Then he asked, "I hope you haven't disturbed my files. They were all brought over here in anticipation of my move in."

Rosalind said, "What a good idea. We could learn a lot reading your files."

The Governor did cry. Then he left. He met immediately with his cabinet as we heard from the radio reports. Then he announced that a vacant school building would be refurbished immediately for emergency housing for all in the building who needed it. In the meantime, they could stay at hotels at state expense. In addition, the new task force on housing had firmly committed itself to creating thousands of new units of low cost housing throughout the state. Some would be for old people and some for everyone. In addition, congregate housing would be developed for those old women and men who wanted to live in community type situations rather than alone.

We cleaned up the building, leaving it a lot cleaner than when we came. We left our curtains and other homey touches to pay for our rent. Before we left, of course, we used the state's 800 lines to call all our friends and relatives around the state. We had nice long chats on our final free calls.

We had a final meeting and decided to continue our Troublemakers, Inc., to monitor the progress on housing and to do other projects which might come up. We used the xerox machines one last time to make copies of letters to all the students' professors and deans asking them to excuse their absence from classes during the occupation. We pointed out that the students had attended our classes and learned a lot from us in them and during our action for rights.

The letters were beautifully typed by one of our retired secretaries who said, "I have so enjoyed working again while in this building that I think I will set up a secretarial service to type for students and correct their spelling and punctuation." The students said they would put her notices on the college bulletin boards.

David promised the students we would come around and visit them even though he was checking into the free hotel and then into the vacant, to-be-refurbished school building. Emily's son-in-law arrived with his truck to transport her and others to free hotels.

But before we all dispersed, we posed for pictures with the Governor. His mother posed with him, too, but then went along to the free hotel. "More fun than the Governor's mansion," she said.

I was asked to be on the *Today Show* and *Good Morning America*, which I didn't think quite fair because all of us had done the action— not just me. But my new male friend and I sure enjoyed the free trip to New York. I made a lot of new friends in the sit-in. So did everyone. Bob, our reporter, got a raise and got nominated for a journalism prize for getting the scoop regarding our takeover.

Rosalind realized she had leadership abilities and ran for state representative from her district. We all got out the vote, and she got elected.

The Governor sent her a letter of congratulations and said he looked forward to working with her. She sent him back a note saying she looked forward to keeping an eye on housing in the state. She also crocheted him a nice little replica of our housing flag so he could hang it in his reclaimed office and remember us.

Troublemakers, Inc., has a lot of ideas of what to do next. You'll probably read about it in the papers when our time is ripe and ready. Some day, with any luck, you'll be one of us.

CHAPTER THREE

Real Life Outrageousness

IN THE LAST CHAPTER, I presented a fictional example of outrageousness. However, I do not simply fantasize or fictionalize about being outrageous. I live out being outrageous as you can too. In this chapter, I want to give you some personal examples of how I reacted outrageously so that you will get the idea of taking action when it's warranted.

Actually, I did not wait until sixty to be outrageous though it is fine to start then or later. At 55, in training to be an outrageous old woman, I took action.

In August, 1980, I went to a large suburban shopping mall in Newton, Massachusetts, to buy a baby gift for a friend's new granddaughter. I chose a large department store, Filene's, one of a chain. Some remodeling was underway inside, and I passed a huge temporary construction wall which had been decorated with three huge wall-size posters. Imagine my shock to see that they were scenes from old silent films of women being abused. In one, a woman was tied to a railroad track with a man hitting her with a mallet. A second was of a woman on a torture device that was pulling her apart. In a third, a woman was begging her husband to let her go out of the house. They were not identified as scenes from movies—just hung there.

My first reaction was of shock that woman-abuse should be displayed at all. Certainly it was unforgivable that a store which makes millions on women should have the callousness to see such pictures as amusing. Violence toward women and wives is endemic in American society. The last thing little boys needed to see as they went to get back-to-school clothes was women being abused. (They would not know

17

they were very old silent films.) It is this kind of insidious legitimation and suggestion that corrupts the unconscious, creates fantasies, and encourages battering and rape.

Naturally I had to act. But I wished to act in a way that would have the most impact. There are two things I want to do as an older feminist. One is to advocate. The second is to teach other and younger women to work for change. So my first step was to talk to all saleswomen in the area about the posters. I asked them if they liked them, and they each said, no, the signs certainly were not amusing. Then I asked them if they had said anything about the signs, which had been there for some time. They all said no, they did not know what they could do. I told them to watch me.

I asked one saleswoman to use the store phone in her booth to call the general manager's office. I said, "Say, a customer wants to see him on a most urgent complaint." Soon, I heard the store's paging system calling the manager.

He arrived eventually wanting to know "my problem." I explained to him that pictures of woman abuse were obscene, destructive, and suggestive. I told him his daughter and mine could not walk safely in many parts of this country, and Filene's should not be adding to the indoctrination for violence against women. I stated that if the pictures were not gone in 24 hours, I would have 100 women in the store picketing and would invite the media to watch. He said he didn't like being threatened. I gave him my card and said I would wait to hear what Filene's decided. I showed him the bag with the baby gift and said my friends and I had been good customers up until now.

Then I went to talk with the saleswomen, who had been carefully watching and, I hope, learning. Within five minutes, the executive returned with a workman and took down the signs.

I thanked the executive and told him I usually charge for advising businesses on how to meet the needs of women consumers, but this one was free.

I gave my card to the saleswomen and told them if they ever needed help or coaching to call. We older women can set an example for younger women to keep up the battle. Additionally, I followed up with a letter to the main office of the chain thanking them for their cooperation in this matter but pointing out that they need to be more sensitive in the future.

Finally, I wrote an article, published in the April–May 1981 *Broomstick* and republished in *Broomstick* in 1985 and now here, so that other women could learn how to protest.

When you succeed, as I did in the department store case, it gives you courage to go on being outrageous. Ten years later, for example, I did not just seethe when I found in my physician's office a pamphlet from the Massachusetts Medical Society which explained how to talk to your doctor. The pamphlet had several token he's and she's and then went on for three pages referring to the physician as he. I circled the forty plus he's and several token he's and she's and sent a letter immediately to the president of the Massachusetts Medical Society enclosing the sexist pamphlet. I pointed out that in an era when we should be encouraging young women to enter medical school and should celebrate the achievements of women physicians, it was not appropriate to refer to doctors, almost exclusively, as he.

William M. McDermott, Jr., M.D., the Executive Vice President, replied, "We stand humbly corrected. The pamphlet which you so kindly provided must have slipped by our increasingly sensitive editorial pencil. In a profession in which almost 30% of its practitioners are women, it is inexcusable to be so egregious in our presentation. My only defense/excuse is that the pamphlet in question was printed prior to 1986. I hope we have improved since then. Again, I can only apologize."

I doubt very much if that pamphlet will be reprinted without proper revisions.

Being an advocate for women is one way of being outrageous, but you can also be outrageous just to have a good time for yourself. I love to swim and happen to believe that oceans, lakes, and the still-clean rivers left should belong to everyone, not just to the rich who own waterfront property or who belong to expensive beach clubs. It enrages me when I want to swim but am barred because of rules that have to do with money rather than safety or equal access to nature's bounty. I also don't think it fair that the hotels I can afford don't have swimming pools while fancy ones have swimming pools that few people use. So I am adept at crashing, and the nice thing about old age is that nobody ever stops me.

A few years ago, when I was more inhibited, I wrote about my swimming hobby in my book *Out of Their Mouths* (American Studies Press, Tampa, Florida, 1988). I disguised my identity and called myself Bessie, The Phantom Swimmer. Now, at 70, I have the guts to uncloset. Here's what Bessie said and what Ruth does.

*
* *

BESSIE

I am Bessie, the phantom swimmer.

I love traveling but haven't much money.

I stay at youth hostels for $6 a night or at the cheapest motels, but I swim in the best hotels, country clubs, and private beach fronts everywhere I go.

They said that the Boca Raton Hotel and Country Club could not be crashed; I have a cake of soap to prove I swam and changed there.

But the pool wasn't as nice as the one in Phoenix at the Biltmore Hotel designed by Frank Lloyd Wright, with wonderful flower gardens, nice poolside cabanas, fluffy towels, hot showers, and even free snacks. I felt I owed the Biltmore something so I had their Sunday brunch which was expensive, but I packed a nice little supper from it to take back to my $6 a night Phoenix Youth Hostel.

Nobody has ever challenged me.

I don't hurt anything; I give the pools class.

Half the time nobody uses the water. Folks just sit around showing off tans, designer bathing suits, and hairdos they don't wet. My bathing suit was $14.95, reduced in the discount store, and my hair is drip dry just as nature intended.

I have a generic white towel I sling over my shoulder unless the hotel has a different color. In that case, I use my fancy giant colored towel as if I am too much of a hypochondriac to use theirs. I bought that towel for seventy cents at a garage sale.

There is no better cure for winter blues than crashing the best indoor hotel pool in town and helping yourself to a little free coffee and danish from the tables set out for conventions and wasted by those dieters and the blasé.

Top hotels usually have shampoo and skin lotion in the ladies' shower room, but you can't depend on it. Anyway, I like to go to the best department store in town and spray myself with fine French perfume and use moisturizer from the tester bottles.

I thought it would be nice to come to this Elderhostel as a change from the Youth Hostels.

By the way, where is the nearest hotel with a good swimming pool?

* *
*

As a novice, you may not have the courage to crash at first. I assure you though, that because so many people see old women as invisible, it is easier than you may think. If at first you can't be outrageous and just walk or swim in, you can try the poor old lady scam, as my daughter calls it, of saying you just have to swim because you are stiff with arthritis. Say you are a stranger in town, and someone said you could swim at this beach, and you're hot. Most guards are nice young people who will feel sorry for you and let you swim. My own rule is to swim first and ask later, but, if you feel you must, ask. If you get rejected a few days when you ask, you will then become mad enough to crash the way I do.

I have my favorite spots, especially on Cape Cod in Massachusetts where all too much of the seashore is exclusive or has parking so highly priced that I can't afford it. I have found a dozen hotels all over the Cape with ample parking lots where I leave my modest car and just walk in to have a nice swim at the private beach. One of my favorites has a nice changing house with hot showers and no attendant to turn you away. You learn to find such places. Another has a free shuttle boat which takes hotel guests out to a nice island with a beautiful swimming and walking beach. Nobody has ever questioned my being a guest as indeed I am, though a free one. Once I took three youngsters to this hotel beach, and the fifteen year old managed to get a free watersurfing lesson from the life guard. I felt as if a kid had beaten me at my own game.

Swimming may not be your thing. There may be some other recreation which you are being denied because you don't have the tariff. There are outrageous ways to overcome this. I don't advocate stealing, but I do advocate not letting things go to waste. It is my custom to buy the cheapest theater tickets, then spot from the top of the top balcony the empty downstairs seats and move to them. Do you get the idea? The seats are only going to waste, and empty seats down front make actors and actresses nervous so you are doing a good deed.

Conventions at hotels and conference centers are great places to amuse yourself in bad weather when you can't walk outdoors. Many conventions have exhibit areas where you can pick up freebies such as pens, blocks of paper, gadgets of various sorts, and candy. I haven't bought a pen in ten years. People at the booths are often lonely; they enjoy having you stop by and chat. Some of the talks at conventions are interesting. You may find yourself learning a lot about worlds new to you. And, as Bessie the Phantom Swimmer said, "the coffee and danish are nice." Sometimes you even get wine and cheese. You give the place class so you are carrying your share of the burden. Often, they will think you are somebody's mother come to see her or him at the convention, and that is okay.

You do have to be careful though. Unexpected things can happen. Once I cruised the exhibits at a medical convention, accepting freebies provided on the spot and signing up for others which would be sent to me. At a booth advertising incontinence products, I signed my name expecting I would get a package which I could give to a friend who uses these. Several weeks later, when I was not home, a truck left on my doorstep twelve huge cartons of these products, blocking my door. They assumed I was a physician who could give out their samples. It was hard to get into my house past the cartons but nothing went to waste. I called a local non-profit nursing home which was delighted to come and take the cartons away for its patients.

At the same medical convention, I also signed up at the decaffeinated coffee exhibit. I didn't have to buy coffee for two years because the company kept sending me samples to give "my patients." When I switched to herbal tea, I was considerate enough to write the company and tell them to stop sending me samples.

Now, you may think me cheap or greedy but remember, older

women are the poorest Americans, especially if we are alone. We worked hard all our lives for no wages as homemakers or low wages as women so we are entitled to all the fringe benefits we can negotiate in old age. That is, as long as we don't hurt anybody. There is so much corporate waste that our few freebies are nothing to worry about.

Incidentally, the greatest source of freebies in the world is the American Association of Retired Persons, 601 E Street, Northwest, Washington, D.C. 20049. Even though the membership dues are low, it is the largest membership organization in the world plus it makes a lot of money from sales of insurance, trips, pharmaceutical, and other products. You can write for a list of publications and order many useful ones free whether or not you are a member. At meetings, AARP gives away wonderful gadgets ranging from magnetic clips for your refrigerator to toiletries. AARP volunteers get wonderful free trips to Washington, D.C., and other places. I know because for several years I was a Women's Initiative spokesperson for AARP. I also served on its Aging and Mental Health Task Force. The great perks include staying at good hotels and building up frequent flyer mileage if you volunteer at the national level for AARP. You can do so by writing to its Talent Bank. In the course of this, you do some good for others as well as for yourself. It is nice, as I did, to be able to go to your niece's wedding in San Francisco with frequent flyer miles earned while volunteering for AARP.

AARP, being a mass membership organization, is rather mainstream. You cannot be very outrageous while volunteering for AARP. If you want to be more radical, you can volunteer for the Older Womens' League (OWL) or Gray Panther which do not have freebies but do have a more radical agenda. Since at our ages, we have little to lose, we can have a great time selecting organizations on the cutting edge for which we will advocate and in which we may participate in outrageous social action. You may not be able to organize your own sit-in against the kind of anti-woman posters I found at Filene's, but you may be able to find an organization which will utilize your talents in an outrageous way. Read your local newspaper and check bulletin boards for ideas.

In the process of advocacy, you will meet other outrageous people who may become friends.

CHAPTER FOUR

Changing Identity

YOUR REACTION to the first three chapters may be, "she's weird. Who needs to be outrageous—not me. I am satisfied with going quietly and traditionally about my life." That is fine if you are happy.

However, you may be thinking that you would like to change, branch out, become adventurous or even flamboyant or outrageous. Maybe you are bored with your old identity, or it is not serving you well. Perhaps you would like to change but don't know how. Perhaps you even feel stuck in a stifling identity. If so, this chapter may be useful. It will describe the process through which people go to change themselves. What I say in discussing identity comes out of my sociological research and my work in developing theory. A preliminary version of my identity scheme was presented in 1990 at the Theological Opportunities Program at the Harvard University Divinity School.

Although some people go through life with rather stable identities, many of us these days seek self change or have change thrust upon us by dramatic events such as divorce, widowhood, financial change, retirement, illness, bereavement, or other disruptions in our ways of being. Even expected and normal events like aging or the death of our parents can precipitate life changes that require adjustments in our sense of who we are. Much of our identity comes from involvement in social networks that confirm who we are and from our locations in family, community, ethnic group, occupation or retirement, social class, religion, gender, or age cohort. Some of these factors, like race, are fixed, but others are surprisingly flexible. For example, people change religions or give them up, pass for being of a different ethnic group, and change social class and occupation. Some even alter their appearance, age, and gender identification by such means as gaining or losing weight, coloring hair, altering ways of dressing and of sexual preference, or even by such drastic means as plastic or sexual surgery.

Some identity change is involuntary, as when others downgrade us and injure our sense of identity by considering us unworthy because we have aged, retired, become disabled, displaced, or poorer. We then have to do repair work to restore our sense of self. This repair work can take many forms including seeking therapy or new ways to enhance our status in the world and, hence, our self esteem and sense of being valuable. Sadly, some people find it very hard to recover from assaults, internalizing the slights. That is, of course, why ageism and other isms are so pernicious. These isms not only decrease opportunities, they assault our sense of I, of identity, making it negative.

Not all identity change, however, is involuntary. Much of it is an attempt to change—conscious or unconscious. The impetus for change can result from precipitors I see as the D factor in life. This D factor may range from discontent or displeasure with being as we are, all the way to being in danger as we are. In between these poles of displeasure and danger are other gradations of dissatisfaction such as discomfort, disturbance, dispiritedness or dysfunction, disequilibrium, disruption, dislocation, dispossession, displacement, dismay, disquiet, dysphoria, and disorganization. All of these D's tend to create depression and anxiety.

The depressed or anxious individual has two choices. She can dig in or she can dig out, perhaps alone and perhaps with help. Diggers-in hug tight to old identities and ways of behaving with more or less success, depending on circumstances. Digging in may require strong, sometimes incredible, defenses and the manipulation or collusion of significant others. A woman must work hard to act her old self and to convince others by a good performance, even a non-functional one. Gratification comes from a sense of the familiar even if it is familiar pain. Diggers-in risk stagnation, but they do not require significant others to alter their perceptions of them nor do they need to alter their self perceptions.

Diggers-in cling to outmoded roles, like protective mothering which is no longer wanted by adult children. These mothers fear the effort and self change necessary to create new roles. They are, in other words, non-copers who try to tread old paths in a new terrain. Some blame their depression on imagined guilts, God's will, fate, old age, or whatever, and see no way out. Non-coping diggers-in receive some secondary gratifications from the stuckness or depression by having relatives, like concerned children, circling with suggestions the diggers-in decline or are scared to follow. It is like the joke about how many martyrs are needed to change a light bulb with the answer none because they would rather sit in the dark which they deserve, they think.

Diggers-out, on the other hand, must venture the unknown with its uncertainty and insecurity. They must risk failure and be able to handle success. They may lose old associates and roles in the process of creating a new self. They may feel alone and must have the strength to bear that aloneness at a time when their self system is changing, creating anxiety. The self they recreate may, in the long run, be more functional, but, in the interim, there is a shakiness and lack of support.

In my first book, *Life After Youth: Female, Forty What Next?* (Beacon Press, Boston, 1979), I described a woman who went back to school at midlife, leaving the bench-sitters in her housing project. The bench-sitters, her chums in the project, were sustaining though not fostering growth. As a late blooming student, she had to give up the support of these neighbors who resented her leaving them. At school, she was out of synch with the young students of a different social class. In the service of mobility, she experienced isolation. This made her wonder who she was and if what she was doing was worth the loneliness.

I related very much to this woman because my experience, while less difficult, also involved losing a network. When I got my B.S. at age 40, my suburban stay-at-home-mother neighbors gave me a party. When I got my M.A. two years later, there were some congratulations. When three years later I got my Ph.D., and began college teaching, there was dead silence because I had gone beyond the scope of my circle.

Digging out is hard, often stressful, work. Not all diggers-out are the same. In my research, I have found three kinds of diggers-out. The first kind are successful self-copers who can dig out themselves. The second type are diggers-out who are assisted-copers, aided by therapists, friends, relatives, groups, etc. The third kind are would-be diggers-out who are frustrated, thwarted, and sabotaged in their coping.

While some women are assisted-copers, others must or prefer to journey unaided to be a different person, or a somewhat different person. All diggers-out, however, must *act* as different people before they *feel* like different people. Unlike professional actors, they have no director though assisted-copers may get some direction, or learn to understudy their role models. Frequently, changers feel like hypocrites because they wear masks or play parts before they have deeply internalized their new identities.

The process of self change, though varying tremendously, has some commonalities for diggers-out. Most of those I have followed have gone through eight phases in the process of change. These eight phases are: (1) involuntary loss or voluntary rejection of the old identity, (2) mourning of the old identity, (3) seeking models or mentors for the new identity, (4) developing and implementing strategies for identity change, (5) seeking confirmation of the new identity by others and self, (6) resisting returning to the old identity, (7) gaining increasing comfort, and even joy, in the new identity, and consolidating it, (8) repeating the process all over as new life contingencies require still more identity change.

I will go over in detail these eight stages with some illustrative material from my work with women, and from my work with myself. In my analysis, I am grateful to my friend, Dr. Theodora Waring, a Quaker minister, chaplain at the New England Baptist Hospital, who, in a workshop, talked about her religious transformation as a process of preparation, initiation, responsiveness, affirmation, and consequences. Since theological views are often at the core of one's sense of self and the universe, there are, I think, striking parallels between the process of our religious change and our change in identity. In both cases, we are influenced to alter in significant ways our sense of being and our sense of connectedness. Changes in both our religious views and in our self system involve internal and external interactions and our willingness to respond. Both may be confirmed or undermined by our networks. Both have serious consequences for our futures.

To be systematic, let me start with stage one, *loss or rejection of the old identity.* This can be self-initiated as with the woman who seeks a divorce or goes back to school in later life. However, it may be forced on a person who is widowed, involuntarily divorced, or retired. It may be crisis-produced or a gradual take over of the D-factor mentioned earlier. Either way, the person who is a digger-out, rather than a digger-in, must make a new life. A new life means change in self as well as change in one's situation.

In my case, at nearly fifty years of age, I rejected my role as an unhappy wife, leaving my husband and home of nearly thirty years to move from the suburb to the city and to a much less affluent life. I am now self-defined and other-defined as a single rather than half of a couple. My sense of place was shattered by leaving my old community. Place is important to identity which is why geographic moves should be considered carefully. The area to which I moved was a transient, largely student one where it was almost impossible for me, a mid-lifer, to be neighbored or to neighbor. I would not have a sense of place again until I bought a house in a stable neighborhood several years later.

You will recall that the second part of the process I listed was *mourning an old identity.* I did that. In an apartment house overlooking dumpsters and with no green space, I missed my gardener and homemaker roles. Even though my marriage had been unhappy for many years, I missed having someone to cook for and refused to cook for myself, subsisting on fast food, cottage cheese, and that sort of fare. I wrote a poem about this which appears in my poetic drama, *Button, Button, Who Has the Button?* (Available from KIT Publishing). I put the poem into the mouth of Mary, a 50 year old divorcee in the play.

> Leaving the suburb and wifehood
> for a cheaper city apartment,
> I moved my plants in first
> so something would greet me.
>
> The first morning I awoke
> at dawn to see the rats' ballet
> a strange and frenzied circle
> beneath my window and said
> "there are worse things than rats."

Strange things were happening to me.
In what is one to believe?
The city screams at you
and you scream back,
finding your voice
someone else's shrill cry.

Even those who stay in an accustomed place sometimes find it hard to recognize themselves. New widows often say they feel like "half a person" because they were so merged with their husbands. Even widows who did not have especially happy marriages often sanctify the deceased and become nostalgic for a wife role that may have been difficult. I am working now with a widow of two years who has been unable to remove, or have removed, any of the clothes or personal possessions of her late husband because, as she says, "having them around means my house continues as it has always been." Of course, many widows go on to have a renaissance of the single rather than the paired self.

Changing from wife to divorcee or widow, or from worker to retiree, is a status passage that involves a kind of death of the self that was. Equally so are other kinds of identity changes that are less often thought to be problematic. Successful weight losers and their friends or relatives often miss the heavier, familiar image.

We have many rituals like retirement parties and coming of certain age parties and housewarmings and funerals to help us say goodbye to the old status and greet the new, but the process is usually not fast though the rituals and celebrations may help.

There are dig-in widows and divorced women who will not go to events because they were always escorted by husbands and would feel and be treated as less valuable now that they are alone. Similarly, there are permanent patients who will not leave a particular therapist or therapy itself because they have absorbed into their role-set the relationship with a therapist. They cannot visualize themselves as alone, without the support of that person. Therapy is often valuable, even life saving, and therapists serve as bridges to a new identity. Yet sometimes therapy goes on endlessly if a patient uses it to try to hang onto an out-moded identity or to mourn it, rather than moving on.

Moving on is what happens in stage three where we *seek mentors and models after whom to pattern the new identity*. Therapists can serve as real or fantasized models to emulate but so can other people who have the attributes to which we aspire. I have done a great deal of work with displaced homemakers, women who were formerly supported by a spouse who is dead, divorced, separated, or disabled. The best way to help such women is to have them hear the stories of women who have made a successful transition.

We live in a time where groups and organizations are widely available for those wishing to meet people with different behaviors, life-styles, and values. The newly single, recovering addicts of all types, the anxious and lonely have access, at least in metropolitan areas, to self help and leader led groups which serve as socialization to a new role and status. Many such organizations and groups serve as mutated, part-time utopian communities which give people in an alienated society a sense of belongingness, pseudo intimacy, and hope. They also provide role models and mentors for those seeking new ways. When I was learning how to be a single, I went to such groups as The Single Life and The Next Step. This was useful in finding out what singles did although I did not necessarily follow the paths provided.

Retirees who do not know quite how to be in this not always highly lauded category greatly benefit from associating with retirees who have been out of the labor market for some time and have developed satis-factory ways of filling time and filling their egos. The new old or new retirees have much to learn. There are many good places to do this learning. Although there are wonderful courses and scenery at Elder-hostels throughout this country and abroad, their greatest value may be in having the old timers show aging ropes to the newcomers. (The catalogue for Elderhostels is free by mail from 75 Federal Street, Boston, MA 02110.)

For many years I have been leading Older Women Surviving and Thriving groups where women can learn skills and gain information. But the most worthwhile part of the experience is what the women learn from each other. Family Service America of Milwaukee, Wisconsin, published my *Older Women Surviving and Thriving* manual in 1987, so that women throughout the country could have instructions and handouts for these groups which serve as entrees to successful functioning in older years. We all need people to show us the way.

Even though there are models and mentors, the woman herself, as the fourth step suggests, must *develop and implement strategies for identity change.* You are familiar with some of these strategies. People sometimes change names, our names being a primary identity handle. Divorcees may go back to maiden names. Uncloseting lesbians will reject family names as patriarchal and take their mothers' names as a last name or coin a new name, Fran Freeperson, for example. For changers, new ways of dressing or adornment or message buttons will be adopted and new possessions or different home decorations will proclaim differences from old lifestyles. Outward symbols will signal or seek to promote psychological changes. Changers will select an auto different from those previously driven; new relationships will be sought. Hair styles will change, and vocabulary. New activities will be tried. Some of this can be fun; some can be frightening. All of it, and many other strategies, are in the service of a kind of rebirth. The rebirth, like any birth, takes time and labor.

One woman who became divorced chose to move into a group house where all her roommates were single and considerably younger. In this way, she removed herself from the Noah's Ark, two by two, coupled configuration of her previous community. Her strategy provided her with ready-at-hand models. She also found a job, a change from her previous full time homemaking. She signed up for a course at an adult education center, too, where she would have the opportunity to meet people who would know her as a single, rather than as part of a couple. All these efforts helped her establish her new identity. Eventually, when she felt secure in her new status, she was able to buy a condo and live alone. The group house had been a transition device supporting her in singleness and preventing loneliness until she felt secure enough to be alone in housing.

I have had to develop strategies as I have moved into my different identities. For a long time, as a professor, I depended upon the instant gratification from teaching and the companionship of colleagues. I felt needed and important because I was meeting classes, advising students, and performing other faculty tasks. Even when I retired at 65, I continued to teach part time because my students and audiences assured me I was who I aspired to be. Then, I took off a semester from all tasks in order to write this book. Without my teaching/speaking roles, I began to wonder who I was. I felt that having time to write and think was a luxury I did not deserve and felt uneasy and even guilty. Work having always been important to me, I had to adjust my thinking to see myself as a full time writer rather than someone who had crowded five other books around the edges of other kinds of work. So I had to develop some strategies to support my new identity. What I did was to go to a meeting of the International Women's Writing Guild and stand up and ask if any folks in the area where I lived would be interested in a writers' group. Four women were and meeting with them on a regular basis helped me see myself as a full time writer. I also applied for, and received, a residency at an artists' and writers' colony. This strategy also put me in a situation where others were writing or doing visual arts full time which legitimated such activity as worthwhile.

Being in a writers' group and receiving a residency at an artists' colony also helped me with the fifth stage in the process which is *seeking confirmation from others and self that the new identity is recognizable.* This is a difficult stage. Other people are busy with their own lives and struggles. In addition, others may have a vested interest in having role partners and significant others stay the same. If *you* change, this may startle or inconvenience them or require changes in *their* behavior they may not care to make. It is hard to be an activist elder when your children want you to be a nurturing Mom or Grandmother. It is hard to wring out of people that you are what you aspire to be, especially since remnants of your old identity cling to you. We have a history, and others know our history, especially significant others like our parents, children, spouses, lovers, and old friends. We proclaim we wish to change or have changed, and they proclaim we are the person to whom they were accustomed. They may even try to sabotage our efforts to behave in new ways. This is especially true for women nurturers who met other needs.

That is why our strategies for change must often mean moving into new settings with new people who will accept us for what we are now, having no prior knowledge of us. We are more successful, usually, in playing new roles in new settings than in trying to rewrite old scenes. It takes a long time to trust the changes one has made, and we must be careful not to subject ourselves to situations that will call out old patterns. All of us who have dieted know how afraid we are to begin to eat certain foods for fear we will gorge on them as we used to. We may avoid temptation by avoiding restaurants where these foods are featured. In the same way, we may need to avoid people who want us not to change and to seek out people who will like and respect the remade self. This confirms and makes comfortable the new identity.

Phase six is *resisting being pulled back to the old identity*. There is always a pull to our past and the familiar no matter how painful it was. One woman who had established a happy life after her divorce dreaded going back to the town where she had resided with her husband because people there constantly reminded her of her past. Even the buildings and town landmarks called out memories that evoked her old self. Empty nesters whose adult children return to live in the family home because of divorce, monetary considerations, or other reasons find it difficult. Both parents and children regress to old roles and conflict erupts. The adult children feel the parents are pushing them back into dependency, and the parents have to fight the temptation to exercise control. At the same time, the children find themselves seeking from parents what is not appropriate for adults to want. They hate themselves for this and project this self-disgust onto the parents. It is a no-win situation in most cases because old selves crowd new ones. Those with new roles need constant confirmation by the world and by significant others that they have passed on successfully.

Some adult parents can live amiably with adult children and grandchildren, and, indeed, for single parents these days, this is often a survival mechanism. Others cannot handle the situation. Perhaps those parents for whom the return is a return to no longer appropriate reciprocal roles need a support group I would call Support, Cooperation, Reinforcement, and Management to provide the acronym SCRAM. It is indeed hard, when you have achieved freedom from an old identity, to have to return to it. That is also why most older adults in this society will tell you that what they fear most is not death or old age itself but the possibility of dependency, a regression from adult independence to the childlike identity of the helpless.

The seventh stage is *gaining comfort and even joy in the new status*. Not all achieve this, but I truly believe it is possible. In my research and personal life, .I have seen many older women move from nurturing roles as wives and mothers to other roles such as advocacy. In my first book, *Life After Youth: Female, Forty What Next?* (Beacon Press, Boston, 1979), I studied hundreds of women from forty to death and found that, although each woman is unique, there are basically ten types of older women. These types are: (1) nurturers, women primarily interested in giving loving service to others, (2) unutilized nurturers, women who had lost the object of nurturance, (3) re-engaged nurturers, or women who had found new people to nurture, (4) chum networkers and leisurists, or women whose friendships and hobbies were most important even though they might have work and family, also, (5) careerists, whose current or past work was all important, (6) seekers, or women in transition looking for new selves and situations, (7) faded beauties, women so invested in appearance that their major energy went to fighting the aging process or mourning what they conceived of as lost beauty, (8) doctorers, women who ran from healer to healer looking for attention and ways to blame their losses on ill health, (9) escapists and isolates, women who resorted to drugs or alcohol to deal with depression, losses, ageism and sexism, and life tragedies, and (10) advocates and assertive older women, who worked to make lives better for themselves and others. In this book, I fictionalized and consolidated the stories of many women, and, after it was published, I received a great many letters from women who saw themselves in these roles. Those who were in unfortunate roles wanted to change in many cases, and, in many cases, I am sure they have. As I have followed the original women I studied over the last ten years, I have seen many of them move from one identity to another.

As time has passed, they have consolidated the new selves and feel at home with them. I have seen unutilized nurturers re-engage in nurturing through paid or volunteer work or learn how to nurture themselves, something, at an earlier stage, they would have thought of as selfish. I have also seen many of the escapists and isolates assisted to become copers and even assertive advocates or careerists. With a little luck and lots of effort, almost anything is possible if you are firm and outrageous enough in establishing your new identity.

Though we may work hard at creating new identities, the process may never be done once and for all. Social change in our society is so rapid, and women live so long, that we are subject to stage eight which is *repeating the whole process of change*. Bright people, people with potential for growth, may have to change numerous times. We have to go through the various phases of rebirth and recreate ourselves again and again. We always take with us into our new identities some values, strengths, and accomplishments from our old, but we also have to reject some of our old ways.

What I think we take most valuably into our new identity is not old structures but rather the learned capacity for creative growth. We grow in skill and wisdom to find helpful people and viable strategies for change. We also grow to help others do this work by modeling for them and encouraging them. My dear daughter, Edith, calls me a megamentor. I can do this precisely because I have had to make so many changes. I have learned that, unfortunately, anxiety is prerequisite to growth, and sometimes depression is, too. It is only when we become uncomfortable with our old selves, when the D-factor discussed earlier erupts, interrupts, or corrupts that we move on. We may go through some unpleasant times that force the need for change. We may be rather lost while we change, but the change can be productive of a better life.

If you want to change identity, I cannot offer you security. You become a survivor with a sense of accomplishment when you learn how to negotiate your way into better selfhood and better situations. I have had some good helpers along the way, and I hope you will. Watch out for charlatans, but there are good therapists, good models, and good friends available. (See future chapters for guides.)

Some questions you may want to think about are: (1) are you satisfied with your current identity? If you are really happy, you should be. If you are settling for misery, you need to ask why you are a noncoper and how could you cope better? (2) Can you do it alone or do you need assistance? What are the best sources of assistance? (3) Are you a digger-in or a digger-out? Is it better to be a digger-in or digger-out for you? (4) Have you gone through any or all of the stages mentioned here? Are there other stages for you? (5) If you want to change, what models, mentors, exist for you, and what strategies can you develop and implement?

Here is an acrostic about identity that may help you to think about how you got to be who you are and how you could change if you wish to change.

Some Sources of Identity

I am (and you also)
D erived from family
E mbedded in a community
N ot isolated from prevailing values
T hough having unique experiences
I n certain roles and statuses
T aught, socialized, gendered, sanctioned
Y et with freedom to change myself and society.

CHAPTER FIVE

New Selves

THE LAST CHAPTER presented a theoretical scheme of the process of identity change. Clearly, each individual is unique. Not all women follow the model presented. It is much easier to understand how people change from looking at concrete examples. In this chapter, consequently, I will start with stories of women who changed.

I have known many women like the one whose story I will tell first. I have deliberately made up the details of the story so that no woman's privacy is invaded. Let us say her name is Estelle Peters who married at age 23 after working for five years as a secretary. She and her husband, John Peters, had three children. Estelle stayed at home to care for them as was more customary in earlier decades. Estelle, a bright woman, volunteered in the elementary school library when her children were all in school, and she was also active in her church. She made good friends in her neighborhood and helped an elderly woman next door by doing errands for her. When Estelle's children were in high school, Estelle went back to work as a secretary to help conserve money for the children's college expenses. However, she did not work full time as she wanted to be home early to be available to the children and to prepare a good dinner for the family. When the last child went off to college, Estelle was in her mid forties. She was bored with her secretarial job but felt she had to keep working at it because her wages, low though they were, helped with the heavy expenses of having two children in college at the same time, and a third, just graduated, needing "presents" to help supplement the fellowship at graduate school.

Estelle felt inadequate when her children discussed some of the ideas they were exposed to at college. Although she had read a good deal, she had never gone to college. Most of her reading was fiction. She began to read the textbooks that her children finished and stored in her basement. She began to nurse a dream that someday, when the children were all educated and self supporting, she could save money to go to college herself. It never occurred to her that she could take any money from her husband's income for her own late education. As a matter of fact, she really did not know what her husband's income was. He took care of paying all the major bills and the charge accounts, and she used her secretarial salary to buy groceries and for personal needs. She knew that her husband had investments in both their names and that they filed a joint income tax. Their income tax form was made out by her husband's accountant, and, when she signed it, her husband folded it so she could sign it without seeing the figures on it. Now and then she had a twinge of curiosity about his income but suppressed it because he paid bills promptly, they had a comfortable lifestyle, and she had always felt she did not understand monetary issues. She felt secure that he was saving to meet the children's college expenses and felt good about using her salary to buy groceries, clothes, and gifts for the children, her husband, and relatives.

She knew that her husband's corporation was taking money from his income for retirement. When she needed a new car, her husband picked it out and paid for it. Though Estelle was not able to save anything from her salary, she felt well provided for and proud, nurturer that she was, to contribute her small salary to the family.

It never occurred to her that the work she was doing at home, like cleaning, cooking, laundry, and childcare made it possible for her husband to be the larger earner, and that, therefore, in reality, half of their joint income was hers. She saw her money as what she earned or what he gave her when the children were little before she went back to work. She never asked about his investments, what they were, or what their financial status was. In fact, he balanced her checkbook for her and also decided when they would paint the house or redecorate.

Estelle, in other words, was a dependent wife and uninformed even though she was contributing by her labor in and out of the home to the family welfare. Things might have gone along this way indefinitely except that a tragedy occurred. At least at first, Estelle experienced it as a tragedy. The year their youngest child finished his freshmen year at college, Estelle's husband announced that he had fallen in love with another woman and wanted a divorce. He assured Estelle that he would pay for the rest of the education of the two children still in college though he might want them to switch from the private college they attended to a cheaper state school. He assured Estelle that she could keep the house in return for signing over to him HIS investments which were in both their names. He also told her that, since they had been married for a long time, she could get half his social security when he retired even though he planned to re-marry. (A divorced wife who has been married at least ten years can collect on her ex-husband's social security.)

When Estelle asked him about his pension, he said that would have to be for his new wife. Estelle, of course, had no pension in her secretarial job. She figured she would take half of his social security since her own would be based on low wages, years out of the work force, and part time work. Half of his would probably be more than hers.

Besides being emotionally devastated, Estelle was financially scared. She was a good secretary, but she knew even full time work as a secretary would probably not be enough to pay the mortgage, whatever that was, or the taxes, whatever they were. She was only guessing; she had no figures. He had never told her. She became depressed and immobilized. She cried a lot, lost weight, developed insomnia, stopped getting her hair done to save money, and generally felt like an abandoned bag lady. She needed to change her identity from a wife to a single, but she didn't want to, and she didn't know how.

Fortunately, Estelle, initially a non-coper, became an assisted-coper. Her sister, her friends, and her daughter all insisted she get the best divorce lawyer in town and refuse to sign anything for her husband without the advice of that lawyer. The lawyer pointed out that Estelle was entitled to all records of their joint holdings and their joint income tax statement and helped her to get them. She agreed that Estelle could not support the house on her salary and said she would not have to because her husband had a great deal of money, and she was entitled to a good share. The lawyer also told her that the divorce settlement could include her husband's paying for education for her so that she could ultimately support herself.

"I always wanted to go to college and be a social worker or a teacher," Estelle said, "but I am so devastated now, I don't think I could do it. Being dumped by my husband has made me feel like a nothing. All I can do is cry."

Dorothy, her lawyer, suggested Estelle see a therapist and told her how to find one. Estelle now had to begin her process of involuntary identity change.

She continued to spend considerable energy mourning the lost role as dependent wife, but a therapist and a lot of anger at her husband expedited her moving beyond this phase. Her therapist told her about a support group for divorced women, and there she met models and mentors for her new identity. With the help of her therapist, she began to develop and implement strategies for identity change, and the other divorced women helped with this. She decided to have the lawyer get as much income as she could from her husband, including money for her own college education. She applied and was accepted at college. She told her employer that she would leave her job at the beginning of the summer. She planned to use her children's introductory textbooks to study for the CLEP exams so she could get college credit for these courses.

Her still-married friends rarely invited her to their coupled events, so she made new friends in the divorce support group; these women confirmed her identity. She also had a makeover at the beauty shop, bought some new clothes, and went to singles groups where men asked her to dance and showed her that she was still desirable. In fact, she decided to sell the suburban house and move to a neighborhood closer to school and closer to events she would want to attend.

All this was really not as easy as it sounds. Various times when her former husband called about necessary arrangements, she found her heart leaping with the hope that he had made a mistake, that he would ask her to be his wife again. There was a pull to the identity that had been hers for so long. She found herself buying and cooking much more than one person could eat. She had to resist the impulse to give up on her sometimes difficult college courses and go back to doing the secretarial work at which she had always been competent. It was also hard to learn how to handle her money and deal with banks and charge accounts. Sometimes she longed for the days when her husband had handled all financial decisions.

When her car died and she had to buy her first car, she almost called her former husband for advice. She found herself calling her twenty year old son for advice just because he was a male. Then she remembered that he had bought a lemon, taken in by a used car salesman. She asked a new woman friend to go with her, and they got a good deal on a car.

The more she did for herself, the more confident Estelle became. She got good grades in her courses which made her feel she was a worthy person. When she finished college, she would have to make a lot of adjustments to manage a professional job, but her self confidence was growing. She decided to be a social worker and sought out social workers as mentors. They told her she should go on to graduate school for a M.S.W., and she figured she could do so. Estelle had a new identity.

Now Estelle, having been married to a high income man, had many more resources than other displaced homemakers. She also had a good lawyer and a good therapist. Less fortunate women struggle harder and don't always succeed. But Estelle is to be credited. She could have been stuck in non-coping and become an escapist, an isolate, or a doctorer, described in the previous chapter.

One of my publishers, Elizabeth Freeman, also took on a new identity in old age. She had worked for many years as a guidance counsellor. On retirement, she decided to start a press to publish the work of older women, Crones Own Press. Rather than mourn her lost advisees in the school system, she coped by starting a new venture which gave her authors and books to nurture. Now past seventy, she continues to grow and helps her authors to grow, too. I am grateful to her for taking on my poetic drama, not the most popular genre. Other authors are grateful to her, too. I am also grateful to two mid-life women who decided to leave large publishers to become publishers themselves. When Rita McCullough and Sandra Brown started KIT Press, they entered a difficult identity transformation, becoming risk takers.

If you wish to change your identity, you may have to do some mourning, some risk taking, some strategizing, some relapsing, some seeking out of helpers. Only you can decide whether it is worth it, and only you can decide how drastically you want to change.

What is interesting is that a little change can be seductive and make us want more. Estelle started out hoping to graduate from college and ended up with a Master's degree. I also started back to school at age 40, hoping to get a B.S. and teach high school. Then, I felt empowered and went on for the Ph.D., getting that at age 45. A few years later, I got tenure at Boston University. Tenure is something that makes people cling to a position forever, but, in 1982, I left to go to Clark University as department chair. By that time, I was 58. I left Clark at 65 to move on again. I could make these changes because I had learned through life to deal with change and expand my horizons. You can, too.

At the various colleges, I have taught many women who started college at 40, 50, 60, and 70. At Clark University, I directed a Master's thesis for a seventy-plus woman who started at seventy to earn a bachelor's degree and just kept going. Her master's thesis was a wonderful autobiography.

It is never too late for formal education. Most colleges give free tuition to people past 65. Professors love these older students; young students benefit from having them around.

It is also not too late, if you become widowed or divorced late in life, to establish and work on your identity as a vital, important single person. For those who remain married, identity changes may still be in order. When the children are grown, revitalize yourself and your marriage by developing a more interesting post parental self.

Some women find it difficult when their child leaves for college. If you or your friend or your daughter is one of those, you might find useful a set of rules I wrote for such parents.

Ruth's Rules for
Parents Relinquishing Children to College

1   Breathe a sigh of relief. Your greatest responsibility (except financial) is over. You have done a good job raising your son or daughter, as good as anyone can do in these troubled times when the peer group, mass media, and education often have more influence than

parents. It is up to your son or daughter and the college now.

2   Don't call your students; let them call you. Don't panic if you don't hear from them as often as you might like. When they have problems, you will hear. When they need money, you will hear. When they are having a good time with their friends and their growing up, they will put you on the back burner. Don't burn if you are on the back burner. Be happy you raised an independent person who can manage in the greater world. However, do write. Students like to get mail, and you can communicate profoundly through writing.

3   If they do call with homesicknesses, remember that is normal, and there is nothing like coming home at Thanksgiving to cure that. You'll find the generation gap will prevail, and they will be happy to get back to their peers. By second semester, they will be comfortable. So should you be.

4   If you have built your life around your children, now is the time to remember there is life after early parenthood. Develop new interests and friends, or resurrect old ones. If you are a confirmed nurturer, take in a puppy, a kitten, a foster child or do volunteer work in the community for needy children or adults. Your children now need something different from you. They need to see you as able to have a happy life without them. If they feel you are lost and are mourning them, they may feel obliged to develop problems just so you will be needed. Don't make them feel guilty because they *don't* need you. And don't you feel guilty because you don't need them.

5   On the other hand, they are not quite independent yet, and late adolescence is stressful so if they do have problems, be responsive and patient. Growing up takes a long time in our society, and the stresses at college may be different from those of high school. Students must do their work on schedule and do not have teachers or you to nag or cushion.

6   Don't assume professors are out to destroy your student if the student gets bad grades. The student may need time to learn how to manage the work load and may need to catch up in certain academic areas. Often, students who do not do well in terms of grades the first year,

do much better later. Do not be over anxious about grades, and do not ask to see grades unless the student wishes to share. Grades are like personal letters, directed to the receiver, not to the family. Part of being independent is that the student must deal with success or failure in privacy unless he or she chooses to share with you. Competition is harder now. Students who were at the top of their high school classes are now with other top students.

7   Care packages of favorite food are always welcome as are other treats. But do avoid loading your student up with sweets that may spoil appetite for meals. (However, if your student is a generous sort, the treats will be shared so your student will probably not overstuff but simply be queen or king for a day in the dorm.)

8   It may be hard for your student to share a room if he or she had a single room at home. Yet, there is a great deal to be learned by having to be considerate of, and interact with, another person closely.

9   If your student seems changed when he or she comes home the first time, accept the new ways as gracefully as you can. You are probably changing too. Your student has had new experiences and may need to show you that he or she is no longer a child so may exaggerate things. They may also regress when at home because they have been on their best behavior at school, and home is THE place to let down. Don't decide on the basis of one visit home that your child has changed for the worst. Four years is a long time, and a lot of growth and coming back together will occur.

10   Don't be hurt if your child decides on a certain break or vacation to go off with friends. This is an age when young people want to see new things. They know you already, and they are practicing adulthood. Be glad you gave them the strength to leave the safe nest and fly. Even though you would love to have them home, they need *not* to be home sometimes. And admit to yourself, without feeling guilty, the good things about not having them around like peace, quiet, privacy, and less work. You should not be ashamed that you also have needs and wishes apart from those of parenting. Also do not be

shocked if your students are on a different time schedule now. College students get used to late hours.

11 Forgive the temerity of these rules. Nobody can really tell you how to feel or what to do, but maybe something written here will help.

CHAPTER SIX

How to Select Helpers

IN THE LAST CHAPTER, we met Estelle
who got help from a lawyer and a therapist to transit to an independent
woman. It is important to point out that you can be damaged as well
as helped. You must be very careful not to fall into incompetent hands.
Let me demonstrate with two scenes in which women seek help. The
scenes give you both the words and the thoughts of the two participants, a counselor and a woman needing help in both cases. These
women need paid work. Later in the chapter, we will explore two
scenes of women who are older than the first two women and looking
for non-work activities.

Scene One

MR. KLUTZ: Hello, what are you looking for? (He thinks, I wonder
how long this will take.)

MRS. DIVORCED: My husband just dumped me, and I need a job. (She
thinks, please, please help.)

MR. KLUTZ: How old are you? What kind of work can you do? How
much money do you want? (He thinks, I bet I know why her husband dumped her—she's a real dog.)

MRS. DIVORCED: I guess I am too old to get a job. I don't know what
kind of work I can do. I don't know how much they pay. I don't
know anything. That's why I am here. She starts to cry. (She thinks,
maybe I'd better kill myself. Nobody thinks I'm worth anything.)

MR. KLUTZ: Crying won't help. Here's some kleenex. Have you considered seeing a psychiatrist? You seem pretty upset. (He thinks, how fast can I get her out of here.)

MRS. DIVORCED: I have no money. (She thinks, he thinks I'm crazy. Maybe I am.)

MR. KLUTZ: Why don't you go to the Mental Health Clinic? When you feel better, you can come back to this agency. (He thinks, I hope someone else gets her.)

MRS. DIVORCED: (Between sobs) I need a job. But if you think I am sick, maybe I should go to the clinic. Maybe they'll give me some pills or something. I am so desperate. (She thinks, if this man thinks I am a mess, there is no sense even trying to get a job.)

MR. KLUTZ: Yes, maybe you should do that. But if you have no money at all, maybe you could get a job working at night in the nursing home. They are desperate for help and will take anyone. And when you go to see, don't wear that loud print. (He thinks, well, I have given her some good advice.)

MRS. DIVORCED: I just finished taking care of my dying mother. I don't want to work in a nursing home. This is my best dress. (She thinks, I guess I have no taste. I don't want to work nights.)

MR. KLUTZ: Well, you have to be willing to listen to advice. (He thinks, some people won't cooperate. Well, what can you do?)

MRS. DIVORCED: Well, I guess I better go. (She thinks, but where?)

MR. KLUTZ: Well, yes. Have a nice day. (He thinks, you can't win them all.)

end scene one

Let us look at the same situation, a woman needing a job, but with a different counselor.

Scene Two

MR. YOUNG: Good Morning, Mrs. Lost, How may I help you? (He thinks, she looks like my mother.)

MRS. LOST: My husband dumped me. I need a job. I haven't done paid work for twenty years – since before my first child was born. (She thinks, maybe this kid thinks I am too old.)

MR. YOUNG: To tell the truth, our agency is just beginning to serve displaced homemakers, but you and I can work together to see what is best in your situation. (He thinks, I'm glad I read some displaced homemaker literature last week.)

MRS. LOST: I thought I was one of a kind starting out so late. I never heard of displaced homemakers, but that title sure fits me. (She thinks, maybe other people in my boat have been helped. Maybe this kid can help me.)

MR. YOUNG: Would you please tell me as much of your situation as you feel comfortable sharing? What I should like to know is what kind of education you have had, the paid and volunteer work you have done in the past, and the skills you have developed in your years of homemaking and child rearing. I should also like to know any ideas you have about the kind of job you would like and your economic needs and goals. While you talk, I will make a few notes and will ask you a few questions to help keep you on the track and to make sure we cover everything. You strike me as an intelligent person, and I think if we go through the process, we can together begin to see the direction you should take. (He thinks, if she needs a job immediately, I can use the data I get to help her put together a first resume.)

MRS. LOST: I graduated from high school 27 years ago and . . . She continues her story with encouraging nods and questions from Mr. Young. (She thinks, this is easier than I thought it would be. This man seems to think I have done things through the years and am worth something.)

MR. YOUNG: Thank you for providing that information. As you said what you had been doing over the years, did you, yourself, realize the kinds of expertise you have? (He thinks, I need to build up her self confidence fast because, as she told me, she has had rejection in seeking a job alone as well as from her husband.)

MRS. LOST: Yes, I realized I had done a lot of work around managing a home, training the children, and working in the community. You have to be organized, and I have worked hard even though it was unpaid work. (She thinks, I'm pretty smart but I have no credentials, and it would take years of college to get them. I need money fast.)

MR. YOUNG: We will need more than one interview to explore all the possibilities open to you. We need to think about whether you want to go for short term training, longer education, or get a job right away and try to get some further training so you can advance. We have to assess further your long term goals as compared to your immediate needs. You may also want to become part of a support group of other women in your situation. I will give you some addresses and pamphlets. In the meantime, would you like me to suggest some temporary work so that you could be getting some money and trying out work? (He thinks, there is nothing like that first paycheck to restore self confidence.)

MRS. LOST: Yes, I really would like to earn some money right away, but I want time to figure out what is the best way to go. I didn't realize I had so many options—it is a bit confusing. I am also a little concerned about my unhappy 16 year old if I work full time. (She thinks, I'd like to see what those other displaced homemakers are doing, read the stuff he has, and think a bit.)

MR. YOUNG: Yes, I may have thrown too much at you today. But I want you to know there are choices. (He thinks, next time I might suggest that she see someone at Family Service to deal with the anxiety about the adolescent and her anger about her husband. But I suspect it is more important right now to get her headed toward a paycheck.)

MRS. LOST: I would like the address of the displaced homemaker group you mentioned. Also, I would like to see you again real soon. (She thinks, I feel much better than when I came in. I expected the run around.)

MR. YOUNG: Well let's make an appointment for next week. By then, you should have been started in the temporary agency. (He thinks, I have identified some of her interests and abilities, and I'll be able to do some checking by next week as to what kind of short term and long term training programs there are here for her and what kind of funding she might get. By next week, she may feel comfortable enough with me so she can tell me exactly what her financial situation is. And by next week, I will have done some homework on this case.)

MRS. LOST: Before I go, I'd like to ask you a question. Do you think somehow eventually I could become a social worker? I like to help people. As I told you, I have done volunteer work.

MR. YOUNG: That might be a possibility. But that is a crowded field. I think you owe it to yourself that we explore a number of fields you might enter and the pros and cons. (He thinks, it is going to take skill to show her non-traditional alternatives. This is going to be a challenging case. But this lady has strengths. I have to remember that she may look like my mother, but her mothering days are almost over. I have to figure out where she can really support herself.)

MRS. LOST: I want to thank you very much for your help today and for your interest in setting up another appointment. (She thinks, I hope I don't panic tomorrow.)

MR. YOUNG: If you run into any problems before we meet next week, please feel free to phone. (He thinks, she may need a lifeline if she doesn't connect up with the displaced homemaker group right away.)

MRS. LOST: I'll try not to bother you. (She thinks, I can't let myself get dependent on a 25 year old.)

MR. YOUNG: I know you are doing very well considering your situation, but my job is to try to help a bit. Before you go, I'd like to make one little suggestion. That red print outfit you are wearing is very attractive, but when you go to the temporary agency, I suggest you wear a solid color tailored outfit—sort of their uniform, you know. (He thinks, I wanted to say that earlier but I might have turned her off. I hope she can take it by now.)

MRS. LOST: I'm glad you told me that. I'm not used to dressing for work interviews. (She thinks, maybe I better get a simple haircut too.)

MR. YOUNG: I really have enjoyed meeting you. (I hope that makes up for criticizing her clothes.)

MRS. LOST: You are pretty smart for someone the age of my son. (She thinks, I think I'll go to the library and see what I can find out about the job market. After all, I can do a little something for myself and show this fellow we old hens aren't so dumb after all. Next time I come in, I'll have some ideas to bounce off him.)

end scene two

Points on Scene One

Mr. Klutz set the scene for Mrs. Divorced's tears by undermining her self-respect and dignity. He fired questions at her that implied she was not employable, and this became a self-fulfilling prophecy. He did not make any effort to seek resources for her, and she went away in worse shape than when she arrived.

Points on Scene Two

Although Mr. Young is a beginning vocational counsellor, he has learned his profession well. In this initial interview, he established rapport with his client. He has also done a number of other things that are good practice with a client of any age.

1. He treated his client as a working partner, not a passive recipient of questions or of information. He let her tell her own story though he gave a structure to this and elicited necessary information.

2. He respected his client's strengths and showed this respect.

3. He informed the client that her problem, in this case being a displaced homemaker, was not unique though the client herself was a unique and valued person. Thus, he offered the client the concept of being part of a to-be-helped category as a substitute for notions of personal failure and individual crisis.

4. He shared with the client that he was not expert on her particular category's problems but that he was willing to get information, direct her to resources, and work with her.

5. Recognizing the truth in four above, his lack of knowledge, he was prepared to follow through and get information.

6. He took some immediate action (referring her to the temporary agency) but did not jump to a complete and perhaps premature conclusion on the first interview. He allowed for further exploration.

7. He deferred action (suggesting the Family Service agency or

probing finances) until she knew him better, had some money, and could handle this suggestion.

8. He did not squelch her suggestion of an overcrowded career (social work), but he did tell her to defer decision until she had a chance to explore other, possibly more viable, alternatives.

9. He set up another appointment and gave permission to call before then if there were a crisis.

10. When he did make a specific suggestion (regarding dress), he tried to avoid criticism and to retain the client's dignity and self-esteem.

11. He decided to do careful research so that he could move as quickly as possible with this client. He did not wish to push her more than she could handle, but he did intend to push himself. He was willing to get advice about resources.

Now let us look at two women who are older than those in the first two scenes and at their experience with helpers. The first woman, a 70 year old widow, is feeling lonely and depressed. She goes to her physician, an internist, for help.

Scene One

DOCTOR: Hello, Mary. What brings you here today? (He thinks, she looks old and haggard.)

MARY: Doctor, I just don't feel like myself these days. I'm not sleeping well. I am tired all the time. I just can't get used to living alone since Ben died, and I miss him so. I don't seem to do much with my days. I am no good to anybody not even to myself. My house is a mess. I forget things. Do you think I am getting Alzheimer's disease? (She thinks, I hope he doesn't think I am crazy.)

DOCTOR: Mary, you know I gave you a good checkup a couple of months ago. You are okay physically. A lot of widows get depressed, but Ben has been gone two years now. You have to pull yourself together. (He thinks, with the cost of my office expenses and malpractice insurance I have to schedule visits like this that are not full check ups every 15 minutes, so I had better get her out of here fast, or the waiting room will back up.)

MARY: I am really ashamed of myself but I really can't seem to pull myself up by my boot straps. I thought you might help me. I didn't know where else to turn. I don't like to burden my children or my friends. Anyway, most of my friends still have their husbands, and they are too busy to spend time with me. They don't understand. (She starts to cry.) (She thinks, maybe I do have Alzheimer's, and he doesn't want to tell me. He didn't say anything about that.)

DOCTOR: I'll tell you what we are doing to do, Mary. I am going to give you a prescription for something to help you sleep at night. And I am also going to give you a prescription for something to take during the day that will help your moodiness. If you get some rest and have a little help from the other pill, you should feel much better. (He thinks, if she were younger I might suggest therapy, but the medication will probably do the trick.) He writes the prescriptions and hands them to her. As he hands her the prescriptions, he says "Maybe you expect too much from yourself. You are no young chicken, you know."

MARY: Doctor, I really don't like to take a lot of medication. (She thinks, he must think I am really badly off. Perhaps I am. Perhaps it is Alzheimer's.)

DOCTOR: Now Mary, I am the doctor. Be a good girl, and give these pills a try. They are really quite mild. (He thinks, maybe if I stand and walk her to the door, she will leave. He does so.)

MARY: Thank you doctor. Do the pills have any side effects?

DOCTOR: Mary, don't worry so much. Everything will be okay. (He pats her on the shoulder as he opens the door for her and beckons in the next patient. As Mary leaves, he thinks, I'm glad I don't have many geriatric patients.)

Scene Two

Eleanor, also a seventy year old widow, goes to her physician, also an internist.

DOCTOR: Hello, Eleanor. The secretary said you called and said you were depressed. I had her schedule you as my last patient of the day so that we could have time to explore what is wrong with you. I am not surprised you are still having trouble. It takes many widows a very long time to deal with their great loss. (She thinks,

Eleanor looks very withdrawn and unlike the vital seventy year olds I see around. She looks worse than many of my eighty and ninety year olds.)

ELEANOR: Yes, I can't seem to pull myself together. I forget things, don't get much done, am tired, don't sleep well, my house is a mess. Do you think I have Alzheimer's? (She thinks, the doctor looks as if she cares about me.)

DOCTOR: You definitely don't have Alzheimer, and all the tests we took at your last check up show you are physically okay. You are depressed, and it's no wonder, but depression is curable. (She thinks, I am glad I have been reading some literature on widows because I think I can be helpful to her.)

ELEANOR: What do I do to stop the depression? (She thinks, thank God it is not Alzheimer. What a relief.)

DOCTOR: The first thing I suggest you do is join a widow support group. There is one in this town. Here is a pamphlet about it. (Doctor thinks, I hope she accepts this now.)

ELEANOR: Oh, yes, you told me about this when Ralph died. So did my minister, but I didn't think then I wanted to be with a bunch of widows. After all, I had my old friends. But, you know, they are so busy with their husbands, and they don't seem to invite me when they have couples over. (She thinks, maybe I will try this group now.)

DOCTOR: Maybe it is time to make some new friends. You are an interesting, wonderful woman, and there are lots of women who would enjoy your company. You might even consider having another woman or two come live with you. With the cost of heating and all, it must be hard to keep up that big house. The house must also have a lot of reminders of your dear husband. Maybe you would enjoy living in a retirement community where there are activities. (She thinks, maybe I am throwing too much at her.)

ELEANOR: Doctor, that is a lot to think about. (She thinks, how could I live with other people? How could I move? I feel overwhelmed.)

DOCTOR: You know, Eleanor, I have an idea. There is a wonderful social worker at Family Service who has been very helpful to women like you who have to make a new life after widowhood. If you find you need more help than the widows' group, you could see her. Your health insurance will cover her fees. I'll write her name and phone on my prescription pad, and you can think about seeing her. In the meantime, if you find it helpful, you can come back and see me. (She thinks, I better leave the door open in case this doesn't work and I have to try something else, maybe even medications.)

ELEANOR: What shall I do in the meantime about not sleeping? (She thinks maybe I should get some sleeping pills before I leave.)

DOCTOR: Eleanor, how much exercise do you get? How much coffee do you drink? What time do you get to bed? (She thinks, I am not going to give her sleeping meds at this point before trying some life-style changes.)

ELEANOR: Well, I haven't really gotten any exercise for a long time. I drink a lot of coffee and tea to try to perk up and because I don't much feel like eating alone. I go to bed at ten and try to stay in bed until at least six, but I just toss and turn and get more depressed because I can't sleep. (She thinks, guess I'm not doing things right.)

DOCTOR: Eleanor, I want you to take a walk every day—a good long one. Or go and swim at the YWCA. If it is bad outdoors, go walk in a shopping mall. Also, I want you to sign up for the hot lunch at the senior center. There are some nice people who eat there rather than eating alone, and you'll get a cheap well balanced meal. They even have a van to get you if you don't feel like driving. At home, I want you to have some nourishing snacks, not just coffee and tea which prevent your sleeping. And I don't want you to go to bed until you are ready to sleep. Stay up and watch the late shows on T.V., read, do chores, or whatever until you get sleepy. We don't necessarily need eight hours of sleep when we are older. Try to find meetings and events to go to at night, maybe with new friends you will meet in the widows' group. (The doctor thinks, well let's hope she takes that okay.)

ELEANOR: Thank you for caring about me, doctor. You are right. I'll try to do the things you suggested. Maybe I'll think of things myself. (She smiles.) I'm not so dumb, you know. Maybe it is time for me to go back to the volunteer work I did before Ralph got sick, and I had to stop. Goodbye doctor, I'll let you go now. Thanks for seeing me so late so you could take time with me. I am grateful to you.

end scene

As you have seen, Eleanor's doctor was very different from Mary's. Mary's doctor saw her as old and sought palliative measures rather than restorative and growth ones. His goal for Mary was limited by her age and by his willingness to give of himself. Eleanor's doctor, on the other hand, was not ageist. She had images of vital old people and knew Eleanor could still be functional. She did not load Eleanor up with medications, but, instead, gave her some suggestions for peer group support and professional support in moving from bereavement to inter-actions in the world. Unlike Mary's doctor, Eleanor's doctor had read the literature on widowhood which points out that it takes a long time, and often help, to get over this great loss. One doctor was a non-helper whose medications might well addict his patient. He saw weak-ness in Mary, an older woman, and played to her weaknesses, actually increasing them. He did not respond at all to her question about Alzheimer's which came out of a real fear. He may have not really heard her concern in his hurry, but she deserved reassurance. Eleanor's phy-sician, on the other hand, played to her strengths and did not termi-nate the interview by a quick writing of a prescription but took the time to serve Eleanor as a dignified, valuable, if old, human being.

In my workshops and research, I find very many older women are not well served by physicians. At the end of this chapter, you will find a list of ways to deal with health professionals, reprinted from my manual, *Older Women Surviving and Thriving*. But, in general, from any caregiver, you should expect the kind of dignified, constructive treat-ment provided by Mr. Young rather than Mr. Klutz and Eleanor's doctor rather than Mary's. Competent care creates self confidence. Competent care is especially important in cases of depression in older women. I wrote about this in *Hot Flash*, the newsletter of the National Action Forum for Midlife and Older Women, founded by Jane Por-cino, who took her first gerontology course with me at her midlife. (You can subscribe to the newsletter and get a copy of Dr. Porcino's excellent book *Growing Older, Getting Better: Handbook for the Second Half of Life*, for $35 from National Action Forum for Midlife & Older Women, Box 816, Stony Brook, NY 11790-0609. Or you can subscribe for a year to the newsletter alone. A NAFOW membership is $25.)

Because so many people found my *Hot Flash* article on depression useful, I offer it here with some small changes.

*
* *

Depression in older women can be disabling, leading to self neglect and even to self-destruction. Famous older women like Anne Sexton, the poet, have committed suicide despite the interventions and resources they commanded. Those not prone to depression sometimes have been baffled and even impatient with women who, despite concerns and efforts, seem mired in their gloom and self-destructiveness. They tug at us until we wear out, leaving them the more bereft, and us feeling guilty.

Most women have enough experience or empathy to know how depression feels. For those who do not, I describe it in the speech of Catherine, a midlife woman in my play *Button, Button, Who Has the Button?* Catherine says to her psychiatrist:

> It crawls out of bed with you
> grayer than the darkest morning.
> Even three cups of hot coffee
> and the warm, scented bath
> cannot shake its chill.
> Wherever you may go or run
> it goes along, unwelcomed.
> Reject it, but it shares your day,
> your friends, your food and work,
> its voice louder in stillness
> but heard above all distraction.
> There are those blessed times
> when finally untwined and free
> you celebrate your gratitude

incredulous the parasite persisted
determined never to host again
and all the angrier when
the twin returns to share again
your bed, your day, your strength.

Despite Catherine's continuing depression, her psychiatrist informs her gently that her third party payments for medical insurance have run out. Since Catherine cannot afford the visits, they will have to terminate. Catherine may mobilize her strengths, or she may not. The scene's ending symbolizes both a profit-oriented medical system and the sad fact that despite good recent advances and new drugs, there is a lot we do not know about treating depression. Depression is multi-faceted with many varieties that yield to different approaches.

(My study of older women's methods for coping with depression was supported partially by the Stone Center for Developmental Services and Studies, at Wellesley College.)

There is good evidence that women suffer twice as much depression as men, though there is disagreement about the reason. Some believe the explanations lie in the biology of women, but others, including the Stone Center theorists and I, believe the double depression incidence in women can be linked to the social injury that women experience.

For example, in their excellent paper and tape, *From Depression to Sadness*, Jean Baker Miller, M.D., and Irene Stiver, Ph.D., of the Stone Center, point out that women are often not permitted by society and significant others to feel sad about their real constraints, losses, deprivations, and the discrimination against them. Some, consequently, fall into that black pit of depression that immobilizes them. They may or may not get good therapy.

My work and that of others documents that *aged* women are particularly injured by social and individual oppression. This, coupled with the financial, physical, sexual, and relationship losses in later life, provides cause for despair in old women.

What intrigues me, however, is that while there are many casualties, other old women manage to surmount devastating life situations. My recent work has been to learn how they do this, in the hope that the strategies of successful copers can be shared with other old women and provide models for younger women.

I have seen how women in the most devastating circumstances—like loss of vision or a spouse or an adult child, or a move into a nursing home—find ways of taking care of themselves emotionally. It is fortunate that these women have learned self-help because, as has been well documented, physicians and others are not enamored of helping undervalued old women whose finances and social status are low. And those who seek aid, or have it forced upon them by custodians like nursing home staff, are often medicated in ways that may quiet them, but may diminish their faculties and quality of life. Clearly, there are drugs which can help with certain kinds of depression, and there are physiological conditions (even as simple as poor nutrition) which can cause depression. However, many are depressions generated by the extreme traumas in lives of old women, or their chronic deprivation of stimulation, money, good housing, etc. The amazing thing is not why so many old women are depressed, but how so many old women manage not to be.

Old women have more to teach us than most people know because there is a tendency to discount and tune out old women. This society tends to value, mainly, productivity in the work force and, to a lesser degree, the nurturing function of women. We have not yet learned to value the creativity, courage, and competence required to negotiate the ordinary but devastating frustrations and crises of human experience.

Let me tell about Mrs. G., a widow with children in distant cities, whose housing is far less than optimum and whose income is low. Near 80, she has many decrements and few assets. But one asset is that she lives on a bus line and is able to buy, at a tiny sum, a bus pass for senior citizens, which allows her unlimited use of the city buses. She tells me:

"I could sit and feel sorry for myself and go stir crazy in my tiny apartment, especially in the winter when I can't walk. Instead, I make myself get up and dressed every morning, and I go to free meetings that I see listed in the paper. I like to be with people and usually learn something. Some days are hard because there are no meetings, so then, I just ride the buses all over the city. I look at people and imagine their lives. Often, I talk to people sharing the seat with me. It is amazing how much you can find out about strangers. I don't feel lonely when out with people. I get good and tired and then go home to my empty apartment feeling content to some degree. I make an effort to get to know people in my building. It is comforting to see people, say 'hello,' pass the time of day."

Mrs. G., once a very active mother and worker, has found a way of filling her days. I suspect that people who see and chat with her feel more positive toward old women and toward their own future aging, because she is well-groomed, cheerful, and alert. In taking care of her own needs, she fulfills a social function, though not in a dramatic way.

Mrs. G., a "mover," is a different type from Catherine whose psychiatrist terminated her for financial reasons. Mrs. G. would never have voluntarily sought out psychiatric help, being of a generation which eschewed this help for "crazy people." Women like Mrs. G. turn to activity, religion, their friends or family when they feel "down."

Women with confidants are less at risk for depression than those without meaningful relationships. The problem is that many women lose significant others through death, divorce, geographic moves, etc. Unlike Mrs. G., some women do not know how to connect with people when discontinuities occur. That is why we need social supports such as the groups outlined in my leaders' manual *Older Women Surviving and Thriving*. Older women can learn how to connect from such valuable books as Jane Porcino's *Growing Older, Getting Better*, or the Siegal and Doress edited volume, *Ourselves Growing Older.*

But with a little help from their friends, most older women manage by their own efforts, and sometimes medical or counseling interventions. We need to find out more about how they do this. I hope you will join me in this work. Please write to me at the Wellesley College Center for Research on Women, Wellesley, Massachusetts, 02181, to share your strategies for coping with depression. Or do research yourself. There is plenty of work in helping our sisters twice at risk for depression. Coming out of depression is wonderful. As one character in *Button, Button* says:

> One day, I was ready to give up what seemed an impossible life. The next day, there was light and air and energy . . . I could exalt again at music and the sight of sun or snow. The papers

I had thrown about could be put in neat and manageable piles. I could do what needed to be done, and what before had seemed a task beyond endurance. I had a life to celebrate. I had myself."

* *
*

Older Women's Strategies for Dealing with Health-Care Professionals

1 Try to see the same person all the time for primary care so that the person will know you and vice versa. Ask your primary-care provider to refer you to specialists if necessary.

2 If you are dissatisfied with your health-care provider, find someone else if at all possible. It is not wise to see someone who is not helpful, whom you may not like, or who does not like you. If you are in a situation where you have no choice, such as in an institution or nursing home, seek assistance from whatever avenue is open to you. Perhaps you can appeal to your medical providers to meet your needs better. Or seek an ombudsperson, someone who is trained as a go-between and problem-solver. Many states now have ombudspersons who visit long-term care facilities in order to check on the welfare of the patients and intervene when problems arise. Another tactic is to ask children, other relatives, or friends to intervene in your behalf. Similarly, a priest, rabbi, or minister might talk to the medical person for you.

3 Write down all the questions you have before you see the doctor. During your visits, write down his or her answers to your questions. Sometimes patients get nervous and forget vital information.

4 When visiting the doctor, bring a bag with you containing all the medications you take, including both prescription and nonprescription items. This is so your doctor or nurse practitioner can see exactly what you take. Sometimes doctors prescribe medicines that duplicate or interact badly with other medicines being taken because they do not know what you are taking. So bring everything you take by mouth, by injection, put on your skin, in your eyes, or elsewhere on or in your body.

5   Tell your health-care provider immediately if you are having bad physical or mental reactions to any treatment. Some heart, blood pressure, and other medications can seriously affect physical functioning and moods. The doctor should be told about such problems. There may be alternative medications he or she can prescribe.

6   Do not ask for more and more medication to sleep. Older persons often require six hours of sleep or less per night. Do not assume something is wrong if you sleep only that much. If you sleep or doze during the day, or don't exercise, that will also affect sleep at night.

7   If you tend to wordiness, bring the doctor a written list of your symptoms and needs.

8   If you have trouble remembering what the doctor says and don't feel you can write it down, bring someone with you.

9   Insist that the doctor take a good history and pay attention to your symptoms. Do not accept his or her saying "It is just your age." Old people are sick because they are sick, not because they are old.

10   During a general checkup or at reasonable intervals, ask your doctor to do a pelvic gynecological examination. All too often doctors neglect this procedure on older women. Very serious, life-threatening illnesses, including uterine or ovarian cancer, can go undetected without a pelvic exam.

11   Do not let any health-care provider blame serious and persistent symptoms merely on your being menopausal or postmenopausal. This happens too often and correctable conditions can be overlooked. You are entitled to a real investigation of your symptoms.

12   If a caregiver treats you like a fool or a child, speak up politely, but firmly, saying, "I have my wits about me. I have a lifetime of experience. It is my body and my health, and I deserve full information about my condition, my treatment, and the likely outcome. I have a right to this. I am not a fool or a child."

13   If a health-care provider calls you by your first name and you do not like this, say politely, "I prefer to be called Mrs.____ or Miss ____

or Ms. ____." Conversely, if the provider is more formal than you prefer, ask to be called by your first name.

14 When medication is prescribed, ask what possible side effects to watch for, how long should you take it, how often, and at what time or times. Ask whether there are certain things you should avoid doing or eating while taking it. It is also worth asking if a less expensive, generic brand of the medication is acceptable. Sometimes busy health-care professionals forget to give this information, and it can be important. Your pharmacist may also be helpful in answering such questions.

15 Do not allow your health-care provider to dismiss your sexual questions or needs. You may have to educate that person that older people are sexual too. Or, if that person cannot answer such questions, you may need to seek help elsewhere.

16 Do not allow your health-care professional to give up on you because you are older. You are valuable and deserve the same consideration as someone younger. You may arouse that person's fear of growing old but that is his or her problem, not yours. You are entitled to the same quality of care as anyone of any age.

17 Try to get the health-care provider to see your strengths. Many people tend to show their worst side to their health professionals and thus end up being overmedicated or even rejected. Show your strength and humor. Of course, don't hide problems.

18 Realize that nobody is perfect, including health professionals. If honest, correctable mistakes are made, give the person another chance. Often doctors have to go through a process of trying different treatments to see what works. Be patient and realistic if this is the case. Medical science has many unanswered questions.

19 Accept that doctors cannot cure some things. You may have experienced tragedy and losses or be experiencing acute or chronic illnesses that has no easy solution. Sometimes clergy, social workers, friends, and family can be most helpful. Too often people tend to view doctors as perfect parental figures who can work miracles or can help with everything. They are human like the rest of us.

20   Recognize that a health-care professional who seems gruff or impersonal may be very tired, busy, or have other worries. Moreover, sometimes younger people perceive older people as parental figures and transfer to them, inappropriately, negative feelings about their own parents. Older women may be seen as mothers, even if they never were mothers. In America, some people are ambivalent about or hostile to their mothers and may take this out on older women. Don't take it personally. As a last resort, you might try to say something like, "Look, you are treating me in a way that makes it very hard for me. Perhaps you have personal troubles or are very busy. Perhaps you have not liked some older woman in your life. But I am an individual, not that person. Please do not take it out on me. I have come to you for help."

21   If your English is not good and your caregiver does not speak your native language, try to get someone who can be with you and serve as an interpreter so you will understand your caregiver and vice versa. The interpreter can also explain any special or unusual factors, and this can help the caregiver meet your needs.

22   If you are a member of a minority group and experience discrimination when seeking medical care, contact one of the advocacy groups.

23   Above all, always be honest with your health care provider. If you present incomplete or false information, that person cannot make the best choices for your case.

24   Be courageous and persistent.

25   Realize that these strategies may not be appropriate or effective for every individual in every situation. This is only a brief and partial list. Confer with other older women to develop additional strategies.

CHAPTER SEVEN

Being Creative

IN THE LAST CHAPTER, we saw some helpers and some non-helpers. But certainly we should not underestimate our capacity to help ourselves and be creative.

In our later years, we are re-creating ourselves as seasoned older women. We have reached those years in which we *can* be very creative because we have stored wisdom and experience. We don't have a lot of role models so we *have* to be creative. My favorite button, which I wear most of the time says, "Youth is a gift of nature. Aging is a Work of Art." My friend Douglas Richards of the New Hampshire Division of Elder and Adult Affairs distributed these buttons at a conference. Now, I buy them from him, several hundred at a time, and give them away, or sell them, as my mood and finances dictate, to older people who need to be reminded that we are creative but that we also have to work at it. Douglas invited me to keynote a Creativity in Aging Conference, and for it I composed an acrostic which I would like to share with you (next page).

Creativity does not mean merely that you are artistic. It also means finding creative solutions to personal and societal problems. As seasoned women, we have special talents for this. Nevertheless, it helps to have some suggestions to prime your pump so in this chapter I will give you some concrete suggestions to start you off. You may be using some already, others may be inappropriate for your circumstances or personality, but maybe a few will be useful supplements to your own creative ideas. I will number the suggestions, not in order of importance, but so you can make notes of the numbers you might want to go back to and try to follow.

C apacities increase, not decline
R enaissance after caretaking others
E arly experiences become vivid
A ging is an important universal
T ime is more available in retirement
I ntuition has been developed and tested
V ision about life is clear and concrete
I nfinite resources lie within you
T ruth telling is needed and possible
Y ou are well seasoned, a survivor

I ncreased freedom of expression
N o time to waste

A ging strips away non-essentials
G oals are now realistic and firm
I magination flourishes, individuality too
N othing is as important now as
G iving your earned wisdom to the world

1   Keep a journal of your thoughts, ideas, experiences, resources, and other items of interest to you. In writing, we often make known what we know. Writing forces you to think out your problems and issues and to externalize them. Often, as people look back on their journals, they find out where they are, where they have been, and where they should go. They see change in themselves, and they see their strengths. You are writing for yourself. Don't feel inhibited or try to be a literary giant. Don't worry about spelling, punctuation, style. Just write down what you are feeling, thinking, doing. You will find it helps you to work things through and come to clarity. Such a journal, if you wish to share it, can be a gold mine for those who love you, like your descendants. The experiences of women have, until very recently, been left out of the history books. Your journal, if you wish, can be very valuable to social historians and sociologists. In fact, the Schlesinger Library at Radcliffe College in Cambridge, Massachusetts, and other

women's archives are eager to have women's journals for the use of scholars. But the most important reason to keep a journal is for you. You can find books and workshops on how to keep a journal, but you really don't have to be fancy about it. Just buy a nice notebook and get started writing on a regular schedule, or sporadically, whichever is more comfortable for you.

At some point, you may want to get together with other women who keep journals to read portions of your writings to each other or to write together on a particular topic. This is a wonderful way to deepen relationships with people and to feel heard. Some women in Rhode Island got together to read journals to each other, and eventually they began to do public presentations, sharing their journal writing with other women. They even started a *Journal of Journals*, in which they printed journal excerpts.

You could start a journal writing group at a senior center, in senior housing, at a workplace, among people in your church or other religious unit, or just among friends or people you would like to become your friends.

However, you don't have to get into any of this elaborate stuff. Just start keeping a journal for yourself and see what happens.

2 Write poems. Many of us went to school in days when poems bored us because they were long, archaic, obscure, rhymed, didn't relate to our lives as girls. Now there are wonderful free verse unrhymed poems in which women express themselves and deal with their experiences as women. You can write such poems. They are a wonderful way of expressing yourself and sharing your feelings.

I know this because for several years, I have been teaching poetry writing to older people at workshops at senior centers, conference centers, and at Elderhostels. People who never wrote poems before in their lives, or even read them, suddenly find they enjoy the process of writing and enjoy sharing their work. Some have published their work on friends' mantels or refrigerators since they have put their poetry into birthday or Christmas or other holiday messages. Others have published their poetry in local newspapers, organizational bulletins, and even in national magazines. There are a number of magazines especially geared to publish the work of older persons. These include *Reminisce,*

5400 S. 60th, St. Greendale, WI 53129; *ENCORE,* Celebrating Return of the Crone, 604 Pringle, Suite 91, Galt, CA 95632 and *Bonus Years,* Published by 70 Plus Inc., P.O. Box 4592, Oak Brook, IL 60522; *Passenger: A Journal of Remembrance and Discovery,* University of Baltimore, 1420 North Charles Stree, Baltimore, MD, 21201-5779; and *Poet Magazine,* P.O. Box 54947, Oklahoma City, OK 73154. From time to time, other magazines have special issues for older poets. In your public library, you will find writer's magazines and books such as *The Writer's Market,* which will tell you how to publish your work.

However, many poets find their own ways of sharing their poems locally. Several people in my writing workshops have photocopied books of their poems which they give as much valued gifts to family and friends. Some even sell their books at consignment shops and local gift shops.

Rose Walbash, nearly eighty years old, came to one of my workshops. I suggested that she apply to her local town arts lottery committee for funding to put her poems into a chapbook, small book. She got the funding and made a great many people in her community happy by giving them the book. Other cities and towns have such sources of funding. Your local librarian can help you find them. A useful book is *Writers Have No Age,* Lenore Coberly et al., Haworth Press, Binghamton, New York, 1984.

3   Write other things—your autobiography or family history. When I was at an artists' colony in Lake Forest, Illinois, at the Ragdale Foundation, I participated in a Lake Forest writers group made up of women past 65. One of them was having a marvelous time writing her autobiography, including her courtship. Her children and grandchildren were eagerly awaiting each chapter, and the woman was doing important work, reviewing her life.

Psychiatrist Robert Butler, M.D., whose books on aging are very helpful, suggests that doing a life review is important. We thereby integrate our lives and make meaning of them. What better way to do this than by writing an autobiography or family history. My friend Jane Webb has been having a marvelous time in retirement from teaching by collecting old family documents and pictures and writing a wonderful family history. Her research has taken her all over the country, allowing her to make new friends out of relatives she formerly knew nothing about. Many other kinds of writing (including writing for money) are explained in *Writing After Fifty* by Leonard Knott, Writer's Digest Books, Cincinnati, Ohio.

4   Write people in nursing homes, prisons, rural areas–everywhere. You can express yourself while you are helping an isolated person. Some organizations will give you pen pals abroad.

5   Write letters to your local newspaper. Most papers have a letters to the editor section where you can present your political or other views. The *Boston Globe* also has a *Confidential Chat* column where readers write their problems, seeking advice. Two seventy-plus women I know, Beulah Schrag and Laura Ferguson, have shared their wisdom with writers to this *Confidential Chat*. Letters not printed are forwarded to the person who wrote asking for a response, so writers know their messages will reach the needy one. Beulah, who had a leg amputated, was house bound for a long time, though no longer, and she thus could send her wisdom out in the world even when she could not go herself.

6   Be creative with cooking. Cook something you never cooked before. Try new foods. Too often older women who live alone, as many of us do, eat foods they would never have served their families. They don't want to bother for themselves. Realize you deserve. Indulge yourself. Consider organizing a pot luck to which each woman will bring one thing so everyone will enjoy a wonderful complete meal but only have to make one item. Use your good linens and light candles for your own dinner once in a while. One woman in a new apartment wanted to make friends. She baked a dozen apples and went up and down the corridor, giving them to people. This was a creative use of the oven. Nobody likes to heat a whole oven just to bake one apple.

Women in my area organized a supper club that meets the first Saturday each month. They go together to an inexpensive restaurant. It gives them an outing to look forward to, and they bring new people along, enlarging the friendship network. This avoids the "just one" questions when you ask for a table alone.

7   Go someplace you never went before. Be creative by looking in the newspaper and on bulletin boards for events you might enjoy. Don't be afraid to go alone. You may meet people there. But, if you would rather not go alone, call up someone new and ask her to go. The woman may be delighted.

8   Make your own greeting cards. It doesn't matter if you are not the greatest artist in the world. You give a gift of yourself. The Christmas greetings I enjoyed most in 1990 came from Beulah Schrag, (mentioned in item 5) who has had fun for many years making her own cards, and Pinkie Gordon Lane, the poet laureate of Louisianna, who writes magnificent poetry but chose for fun to send her friends a greeting card with her amateur drawing of a teddy bear sliding on the ice and outlined in pink. The name of this retired Louisianna State College professor is Pinkie.

9   Draw or paint on your clothing for fun. I have already told you about my RASP sweat shirt and Tee shirt which I have had a lot of fun wearing. Hint: painting stuff on your clothes is also a good way to cover stains.

10   Do a creative housecleaning. Get rid of the clutter that is driving you to despair and taking up your time re-arranging. Simplify your life. Live lightly. Give a garage sale to benefit your finances and freedom from possession by possessions. If you are rich, give the garage sale to benefit your favorite charity. Or give away stuff to people who might need it.

11   Read the kinds of books you never read before.

12   Have a library hour or two every day if you are retired. Instead of spending money subscribing to magazines and newspapers and buying books, go to a comfortable public library. Use their heat and air conditioning instead of your own. It will give you a reason to get dressed and out of the house and cost you nothing—indeed save you money over the costs of subscribing. A fringe benefit is that you will probably meet other people doing the same thing and make friends. Don't be afraid to ask someone to go out for coffee. Other people are

lonely and shy too. Rejection will not kill you. Acceptance may delight you.

13 Take a course. They are free – or greatly reduced – for people past 60 in most places. If you are younger than 60, ask to swap chores for the course.

14 Go to an elderhostel or a conference.

15 Take up birding, wildflower spotting, star gazing, sea shell collecting, a hobby that will get you outdoors. It is creative to be involved in the creatings of nature. The air and exercise will do you good and so will the adventure. Get a bird book, star book, flower book, etc., so you will be knowledgeable. Seek out others with the same interests or proselytize to get your friends interested. When you are disgusted with people, go to zoos. They are wonderful. If you need the excuse of a child to go to the zoo, borrow one. In most families, these days, both parents work, and the children don't get too many expeditions.

16 Get a pet. Research shows that people who have had heart attacks recover more quickly if they have a pet. Besides providing companionship, dogs require that we get out and walk. This promotes exercise and the chance to meet people. Hopefully, you haven't had a heart attack, but a pet can still make your life happier. When my dear uncle died, his wonderful wife was terribly lonely living alone. Her son and daughter-in-law and children lovingly spent time with her, but she still had to be alone a great deal. Then, they bought her a dog, a puppy who needed much care but returned the favor by adoring and amusing my aunt. There was always someone to greet her when she came home and to ask to be taken out. It helped.

17 It is very creative to volunteer or to do part time work. There are many opportunities everywhere for volunteering and some for part time or full time jobs for older women (See chapter seventeen). The volunteer work I have done has brought me greater benefits than I have given. Any volunteer will tell you this. Decades after retirement as a social worker, my friend Betty Lindemann helps as a volunteer in inner city Boston schools.

18   Offer services for money or love to young families. Besides taking children on outings as mentioned above, you can read to them, baby sit, teach them crafts or skills. My daughter Edith still remembers how an old woman next door taught her how to tie her shoes, put greens in with flowers, and told her stories about the old days. In Mrs. Proctor, Edith had an extra and valued grandmother. Letty Proctor also taught me much.

In fact, older women can be very influential if they will take the time and put the effort into helping children. Here is a poem I wrote this year, at age 70, about an old woman neighbor who made a tremendous difference in my life.

Goodie of Homestead Street

My tenth summer 55 years ago
we put on plays in Anne's garage.
Kids were three cents; adults five.
I was the author and star
but Anne drew the audience
her sisters, mothers, aunts.

Across the street
my grandmother and aunts
watched my mother perform
her long cancer death drama
filling me with guilt
for childishness, for living.

Goodie, an old woman neighbor
came to all our plays.
She was my special audience
telling me I was a writer
not just the back seat child
of the dark death theater.

Now Boston's Homestead street
is a theater of rage and blood
killings, drug deaths, raids

even the fatal shooting of a
ten year old girl sitting out
the show on a cement stoop.

I might have died there too
if Goodie had not applauded.
Goodie, this is my late encore.
It took half a century
to thank you, a spinster,
who gave me a life.

19 Start a small business.

20 Change your style of dressing to reflect creative you. This does not
have to be expensive. Seek out local thrift shops, rummage sales, garage
sales. People often comment on my interesting, unusual clothes. I get
a lot of them at the Wellesley College Alumnae's annual Clothes Cup-
board, especially the last day when you can fill a huge bag for three
dollars. There are lots of other rummage sales where, on the last day,
you can fill a bag for one dollar, but Wellesley alums have high class
stuff. Even if you don't sew, you can make some wonderful stuff for
yourself. I'm a woman of size so I buy great interesting Guatamalen
fabrics just long enough for a top fold, cut a neck hole and sew up the
side, leaving room for armholes. People ask in which boutique did I
get these wonderful tops. They cost me less than $10. I have also,
though a non-sewer, bought wonderful fabrics at garage sales which
I can treat the same way. My greatest find was for $2, a gorgeous piece
of tie dyed fabric from Nigeria which made a magnificent top. I wear
it when I give poetry readings. People think I went on an African safari
seeking it. They don't know my car stops automatically at garage sales.
Though I don't always buy, I often just have fun meeting the people.
I also have a great collection of garage sale jewelry, so much that I supply earrings to two other women too chicken to get their ears pierced.
Many women are much more creative than I. They make jewelry out
of odds and ends. Perhaps you can. Look around at the old buttons
you cut off discarded clothes. They make creative earrings and neck-
laces. I made a necklace out of the buttons in my Grandmother's in-
herited button jar.

Experiment with different hair dos. Don't get in a rut. Grey hair is beautiful. Treasure it and arrange it well. Wear bright colors to set it off. Black and brown are probably no longer your colors.

21   Take up some kind of handiwork. We need a change from head work. My nearly-70-year-old friend, Martha Gordon, is constantly knitting children's mittens out of discards of yarn people give her. The more boring meetings she goes to, the more she can make. At Christmas, she has dozens of beautiful mittens to give needy children. This gives her much satisfaction. Knitting may not be your thing but maybe you can select some other craft to bring you satisfaction. If nothing else, using your hands for crafts keeps you from using them to nibble on food between meals.

22   Find a creative way of giving charity even if you have no money. As mentioned in 21, Martha knits mittens out of discarded yarn. She has little extra money, but she is a large contributor to Rosie's Place, a shelter for homeless women. She collects the tonic bottles students discard at the Wellesley College Science Center, turning them in for the money which she donates to Rosie's. Martha also collects Science Center styrofoam and recycles it to help the environment.

23   At least once a week, make yourself go to an event that is new for you. Look on the religious pages to see what free events the churches and temples in your area are sponsoring. Though I am not an Episcopalian, I very much enjoyed a recent lecture at the Episcopal Church where I was warmly welcomed. If there is a college or university in your area, be sure to get onto the mailing list for events that are open to the public.

24   Re-arrange your living quarters to reflect your new interests. This does not have to cost much money. You can do a lot with posters, color, and garage sale renaissance.

25   If you love to dance and have no partner, dance alone to music in the privacy of your home. It is good exercise, also.

26   Grow plants and talk to them.

27 Get suggestions from people you meet about fun things to do. Do them.

28 Talk to people on busses, planes, in waiting rooms. My friend Dr. Helen Kenney, a retired professional, met a great new friend with mutual interests while both were waiting in a doctor's office.

29 Write for an American Youth Hostel membership. They have special rates, lower for people over 60. Despite the name, the hostels are not only for youth. The rates are so low, ranging from $6 to $15 a night, that you can afford to travel. There are wonderful hostels all over the United States, many of them in fascinating places. To get a membership and the book-sized directory, write American Youth Hostels, AYH Travel Store, P.O. Box 733 15th Street N.W. Suite 840, Washington, D.C. 20005.

These hostels have fully equipped kitchens. You can cook your own food, another money saver. The wonderful thing is that, at the hostels, you meet young and old people from all over the world. I have sat in the lounges of youth hostels in San Francisco, New Orleans, St. Louis, Rochester, Vermont, Orlando, Florida, and other wonderful places. And there I have met fascinating people and been much happier than in a sterile hotel room.

Probably one of my best trips was to Key West, Florida, the southernmost point in the United States, where I paid $12 a night for a bunk in a youth hostel while people down the street were paying $100 for rooms. I used the same beach they did and even shared their pool. It was within walking distance to many of the wonderful attractions there. I went to that youth hostel directly from an Elderhostel on one of the small keys, or islands, above Key West. We studied the ecology of that beautiful area. Thus, I was having the best of two worlds in two weeks, both a youth hostel and an elderhostel.

30 Think of some creative activities and outlets for yourself. Mine may give you some ideas, or you may have much better thoughts. The main thing is to get out of a rut (if you are in one) and to realize that, in later years, we can be creative about our lives. If you agree, copy my acrostic from the beginning of this chapter, and hang it where you will

see it frequently. That will remind you that you are creative and confront you with the necessity to work at it.

Another way to remind yourself of the potential for growth and creativity is to always have something growing around you. Even sticking a sweet potato or a carrot top in a glass of water to grow green leaves reminds you that all creatures need to grow. As I write this chapter, on the window sill over my desk stands a glass in which I have put one paper narcissus bulb which I bought for fifty cents. It is inching its way up to eventual beautiful blooming. Whenever I get discouraged at the slow hard work of writing, I look at my patient narcissus, whose bud was long dormant until I watered it. I know I can make it grow. And I can make my book grow too. Similarly, with patience, you can make your projects and yourself flower.

CHAPTER EIGHT

House Yourself Creatively

FORTY-FIVE PERCENT of women over 65, and many seasoned women under that age, live alone. Helen Hicks, M.S.W., former director of the Wellesley, MA, Council on Aging, says the question most often asked by older women is, "Since I do not like living alone, but am alone, how do I endure this?"

I answered this question in my Prime Time column in the excellent national women's newspaper, *New Direction for Women*, available from 108 West Palisade Avenue, Englewood, NJ 07631. With the permission of the editors, I am going to start this chapter with that column, originally published in the November/December 1986 issue. In it, I repeat a little of the information from the creativity chapter, but I want to do that to reinforce the youth hostel and Elderhostel opportunities mentioned there.

Here are some suggestions.

Getting Together

First, have you considered not living alone? Many women share housing which creates community, cuts expenses, and provides physical and emotional security. If you have friends in the same situation, get together! If not, seek housemates by contacting social service agencies and the senior center in your area or by placing an ad in your local newspaper.

Four women I know bought a four-apartment building, and, although each has her own quarters, they leave their doors open, eat together frequently, and enjoy knowing friends are nearby. Another group rented a big house where each has her private rooms and shares a kitchen, living room, and outdoor space. In many communities, senior housing and congregate living already exist—it's smart to put your name on their waiting lists as early as possible.

Taking in Boarders

Another possibility is staying in your home and taking in boarders—a person your own age, a professional just starting out, or a student who might do some of the chores.

Listing with a bed and breakfast directory would give you the opportunity for frequent visitors, some income, and the stimulation of meeting new people. One older person I know, who does not need much income but does need diversion, lists her sleeping quarters through American Youth Hostels, P.O. Box 733 15th Street N.W. Suite 840, Washington, D.C. 20005. It serves all ages, traveling Americans as well as visitors from other countries.

Some churches and other religious organizations provide a national directory of members willing to take guests for short periods. If your own group does not, you might want to initiate such a listing on your own.

Be at Home Less

If living with other people is not for you, another solution is to continue to live alone but be at home less. Stay at American Youth Hostels for $5 or $6 a night.

There are also Elderhostel weeks with room and board, interesting courses, recreation, and good companionship for a reasonable fee. Write Elderhostel, 75 Federal Street, Boston, MA 02110.

In addition, airlines, buses, and trains have reduced fares for older people.

Sharing Meals

If you can't travel or don't want to, break your isolation by sharing lunches or dinners (each bringing a dish) or taking turns cooking.

You might ask your religious organization or some other group to set up arrangements for shared meals. Do not be too proud or ageist to patronize existing senior citizen meal sites where you might also have an interesting program.

Community Services

To combat loneliness, take advantage of all community services. Watch your local newspaper for events and attend. If you don't drive, don't be ashamed or hesitant to call and ask for rides.

If my advice seems off target because you have trouble reaching out, or if you know of other women who have trouble making new relationships and finding new ways of living, ask your senior center or other community agency to start an "Older Women Surviving and Thriving" workshop to be led by a professional or a volunteer, perhaps you. One session is devoted to helping work out living arrangements, others to making new friends, sharing wisdom, coming to grips with and accepting your aging, identifying problems, expressing and dealing with feelings of loss, grief and anger, transforming and sharing lives through creativity, managing sexuality and family relations, financial management, health maintenance and medical care, advocacy and community involvement.

Older Women Surviving and Thriving is available for $17.95 plus $2.50 mailing charge from the non-profit social service agency, Family Service America, 11700 West Lake Drive, Milwaukee, WI 53224.

Doing for You

One of the reasons older women hate living alone is that they feel useless if they cannot do for others. Consider reorienting yourself to do for yourself and to feel entitled to that. Indulge yourself and make your home your castle with yourself the queen. Do for yourself what you used to do for others, without guilt and with joy. Don't romanticize how it was to live with others. When you live alone, you can have things your way. You are an important person. You do deserve.

*
* *

Since I wrote that column, I have learned more which I would like to share here. I have had glowing reports from Elizabeth Freeman's project in Durham, N.C. Elizabeth creatively conceived a cooperative apartment house where older women could have privacy in their own apartments and yet have others available for companionship and crisis. It has worked out well as a result of considerable effort from Elizabeth and the women concerned.

Another older woman I know has solved her housing and finance problem in one creative swoop. She saw an ad on a bulletin board offering free room and board in exchange for fifteen hours a week of being available to keep an eye on three school aged children. The ad said the hours were late afternoon and evening. The woman, who loves children, applied for the job. Now, instead of living alone expensively, she lives freely with a nice young family who give her plenty of privacy but also companionship. She has a very large bedroom-sitting room combination and bath in a beautiful home with lovely grounds where she gardens. She is welcome to have guests; her daughter, who lives across the country, stayed with her for a week on a recent visit. She entertained me in the garden of this home, and I was invited by the family to stay for dinner. She has come to love the children and they her. When she is "on duty" the fifteen hours a week, the children are occupied doing homework, watching television, playing with friends, or reading. Now and then, she does have to referee fights between the siblings or make suggestions to the children, but much of the fifteen hours she can simultaneously read or do other things for herself. She has most of her evenings free and does not resent the stay-at-home evenings when she is babysitting.

Now sixty, the woman says, "When these children are too old to need me, I will find another family. If I don't find another bulletin board ad or an ad in the newspaper, I will run my own ad. I also know there are agencies that serve families, and I will seek the help of one to get a new placement. However, even when Jodie, Sara, and Peter grow up, I plan to keep in touch with them and their parents because I feel attached to them."

The parents in this family told me that they consider this woman a Godsend, are grateful for the good care of their children when they are out, and consider the woman a friend they will cherish even when they no longer need childcare. "Maybe she will stay on as a boarder," they suggest "unless we move to a smaller house when the kids leave. Knowing an older woman and benefitting from her wisdom are wonderful because both our parents and the children's grandparents live at such a distance we see them rarely, mostly on holidays."

Incidentally, during the children's school vacation at Christmas, this young family goes for a week to visit one set of Grandparents each year. They encourage their built-in babysitter to use their whole house then, and she always gives a big Christmas Eve pot luck party and invites all her friends. They love it. Most of them live in small apartments and could not entertain the whole network at once.

Another woman does maintain a small cheap apartment but advertises house sitting in local papers in towns and cities near her. For periods of a week to six months, she gets to live in the houses of people who will be away. People who are worried about their houses, plants, pets, and gardens usually have beautiful homes. This adventurous woman has a wonderful time exploring new neighborhoods and living in the luxury she could not afford. She is now planning to put ads in newspapers far from her home so that she can indulge cheaply her yen to live in other parts of the country. She is also thinking of charging a fee for her services. Then she can cover the rent of the apartment she maintains for between times. She has so many excellent references now that she probably can command a good fee. Her fringe benefit is that she has made friends among the people for whom she house sat. A second and important fringe benefit is that she is out of rage about having to live in a tiny cheap apartment. She took an outrageous step that solved her problem.

On her church bulletin board, another woman found a notice from a single mother asking for someone to live with her, at a much reduced rent, in return for some childcare. This also turned out to be an excellent arrangement. The older woman, aged seventy, felt useful helping out the young mother and acquired a surrogate granddaughter. She considered the hours spent babysitting a pleasure and now lives in a better house than the one she was having trouble affording. I think more older woman might consider moving into someone else's home or taking someone into theirs.

For awhile, I had a young cousin from another state living with me while she attended school and worked in the Boston area. I enjoyed getting to know this young woman whom I had hardly known before. Even though she has her own apartment now, we have a closeness that we would never have had, had we not lived together for awhile. Many people have told me that, though having your own adult children live with you has hazards, having someone else's may be more neutral and safer, there being more distance and less subjectivity. Some older women I know have enjoyed living in Y.W.C.A. residences and getting to know the young working women who live there, too.

Many people have enjoyed taking in foreign students who are attending high school or college for a semester or a year in the United States. This is a relatively short term commitment and a good way to get to know something about other cultures. I was well rewarded when I opened my home to a couple and their baby from an under-developed country who were here for advanced education. I helped them until they found a suitable apartment, and they helped me with my guilt over living alone in a house that had room for others. Some people have taken in homeless individuals or families. That is certainly needed now when 40% of the homeless are working people who cannot afford housing. If you are interested in these sorts of arrangements, you can contact social agencies in your area for referrals.

A good place to find students, graduate or undergraduate, or faculty members to live with you is the college housing office or the college bulletin board. You can rent to them or, if you are frail and need someone to do shopping and cleaning, you can swap housing for chores. A widower I met in Williamsburg, VA, uses the housing office of The College of William and Mary to get a young couple, sometimes with children, to live with him while one or both of the parents is at graduate school. He gives them free rent in his big house in return for the companionship and security of having people there. He does not expect them to cook for him, but he finds that when they have a nice meal, they often invite him to join them. Otherwise, he manages on T.V. dinners and easy-to-make things. Widowed or divorced or never married women with big houses in college towns should consider this.

Naturally, you may be afraid of plunging into an arrangement you may not like. Well, you can try it out gradually. Every year, Katie Bank-hart and her husband, a wonderful couple who used to live in a big house in Wellesley, would adopt a foreign student from Wellesley College and have that student stay with them during the college vacations when other students went home. Now they live in a retirement village on Cape Cod so that is no longer possible, but they still have wonderful relationships and correspondence with the students they made welcome.

Helen Hicks of Needham, MA, who has a home with extra space and a limited retirement income from her social worker job, started out by renting a room to a student from Babson College during the academic year. The student took most of her meals at the college and was rarely home. After several years of renting to students who were away from May to September, Helen decided to take a chance on a year round working person. She also decided to extend kitchen privileges. This worked out for Helen, and, in the process, she acquired an answering machine because the working woman she housed had one. She also got some good Chinese food because her housemate was of Chinese origin.

There are many other ways to avoid living alone. Some mature women have taken jobs at colleges as housemothers with nice apartments and many privileges. Two women I know share a job and an apartment in a housing project for the aged that is run by a foundation.

There are so many housing alternatives, you may want to explore them with other women. Mid Life Options for Women, an organization for no longer young women, sponsored an alternative housing exploration workshop for women. You could do this in your area. As a result of this "Mid Life Options" workshop, some women investigated group living on a permanent basis, but others, unexpectedly, worked out group vacations. Eight of the women rented a condo on an island off the coast of Florida and had a wonderful winter vacation. In fact, it was so good that, in the summer, they rented a house on Cape Cod for another group vacation.

Group vacations for women alone are a wonderful way to save money and avert loneliness. For eight years, I was part of a group of twenty-two people who rented an inn for two or three summer weeks on Cape Cod. We did all the cleaning, shopping, and cooking collectively. We bought most of the food wholesale before we went to the Cape or bought it off Cape before we went because it was cheaper. For instance, I would bring down enough bagels to freeze for three weeks from a bagel place. Because I bought so many dozens, I got a great price.

On the first night of our stay, we would have a house meeting where we divided up the chores. Although it was work to cook for 22 people, we had two or three cooks each night. It was fun to cook with others, especially knowing another crew would clean up. We had a few couples in the group, but most people were widowed, divorced, or never married. Since we had some parents, including single parents, our age range was from four to seventy. The inter-generational experience was wonderful.

During the eight years, our group aged, and, by the end, we had no young children, only adolescents. During the years, we also lost members to geographic moves, busyness, re-marriages, death, and wanting something new. But we were always able to find new people eager for a cheap and fun vacation. Many of the people who came to the Cape House lived alone the rest of the year. For them, it was a special treat to come together. During the year, we had reunions and planned pot luck suppers. We Cape Housers had a nice ongoing network.

I made many friends in this group. Though we no longer have the Cape vacations, we have warm memories which we share at our reunions. For example, Sylvia Fee, a generous, warm woman, opens her lovely home to many of us each year for a New Year's day supper. Last year we also had a Fourth of July party attended by a number of Cape Housers.

This Cape House came into my life shortly after I was divorced at fifty. It was wonderful to have a cooperative summer vacation every year. I still laugh thinking of the fun we had nights playing charades and other games, and putting on skits. We had a contest each year to see who could find the most outrageous outfit at the famous Cap Cod thrift shops and rummage sales. When Sylvia adopted a kitten called Scargo from a litter at the Scargo Pottery in Dennis, we gave her a party that supplied everything a cat and its owner would need. People made hilarious and outrageous cards to go with their gifts.

One year, on the last night, we had an award ceremony where everyone got an award for being a "great camper." I bought, and gave, a toilet brush to dear Carol Haley who hated to cook and did her chores cleaning the bathrooms.

What I am suggesting here is that you don't always have to live alone. Even breaking up your solitude with something like the Cape House can make a difference. You can take the lead in organizing something like this. Several people in the Unitarian Church in Midland, Michigan, did just that. They got together and organized a group to buy, and use collectively, a summer house at a nearby lake. I was invited to this house when I was in Midland for one summer at the Alden Dow Creativity Center. It was a highlight of my stay to be at the pot luck meal with good sisterhood and fellowship at the U.U. summer retreat house. What each person could not afford alone, the group *could* afford. It was great fun to get to know people. One person shared a boat, and others brought musical instruments to give pleasure.

Women for whom money is not issue and who have nice homes can register with one of the home exchange programs for people who want to swap homes when traveling. You can find these services advertised in *Modern Maturity*, the AARP magazine, and in other magazines.

Incidentally, in regard to housing upkeep and other housing arrangements, you can write for excellent free pamphlets and booklets to Fulfillment, AARP, 601 E Street, N.W., Washington, D.C. 20049.

In your library, you can find resource books on developments for retirement living. Most areas of the country now have these. Some are profit making, but others are non-profit. Some offer totally independent, retirement apartment living only, along with recreational facilities that are shared. Others have extensive programs, meals, and even guaranteed long term care in a nursing unit if you become needful of that. They vary tremendously in cost and services. Should you be interested in these retirement complexes, investigate carefully, and be sure to ask outrageous questions. Some have deteriorated, gone up in fees; others have failed entirely. People who thought they were set for life have lost their savings and security. Consult your state Department of Elder Affairs and your local council on aging as well as the books in your library on retirement communities.

If you are considering moving out of state, investigate that thoroughly, too. If you relocate, it is very important to find out what elder services exist in the new community because you *are* going to age. There is a reverse migration from some sunbelt areas. People who become frail find the support networks do not exist there for them, and public services are over burdened because there are so many elders. One seventy year old who moved to a sunbelt community made her daughter promise she would put her on a plane and bring her to her old community if she became ill because the medical services are so poor where she is now. But if you become ill, you can't always be transported.

If you consider relocating, find out what opportunities you will have to keep *mentally* active. Are there programs of interest to you? When I was a visiting professor at The College of William and Mary in 1990, I discovered that many people had chosen to retire there because Colonial Williamsburg and the College offer so many enrichment opportunities. In fact, the College has a Town and Gown luncheon every week during the academic year where professors and other fine speakers give interesting talks and lead discussions. I went to those while at William and Mary and discovered that the audience was almost entirely retirees and spouses of retirees. Many of the several hundred attendees were women long past sixty five. Besides getting a good lunch cheaply and an interesting talk, at the social hour before lunch and again at the tables, they had an opportunity to meet people who would become friends. I found that another older woman, Mary Hazzard, a fine novelist who had been a visiting professor in English, has also gone to the lunches to make friends for her year in Williamsburg. It is important to select a new community, if you relocate, that has mechanisms for making friends. My wonderful Aunt Bert Kaplan moved to Florida. She makes friends by talking to people she meets on the beach, in the malls, and even at the events she finds to attend. However, not all of us are so outgoing. We may need a place where interactions are structured for us in the wonderful way the Town and Gown Club does, providing round tables for strangers to meet over lunch.

I hope that, in the future, more ways will evolve for elders to come together besides senior centers. Some people don't consider themselves old enough for senior centers, or they do not enjoy the programming. While I was in Williamsburg, the Williamsburg Inn, part of Colonial Williamsburg, offered free tea and musical entertainment on

Sundays to people over 65, members of their Regency Club. I enjoyed this. I met people there, also.

The town of Weston, Massachusetts, had me teach a writing workshop in one of its elderly housing projects, and it brought the residents together. It was sponsored by the Council on Aging. People from outside the elderly housing also came in to the project to attend the workshop, thereby extending the friendship network. Perhaps you can organize a project in housing that is mostly for older women.

What I have been suggesting in this chapter is that you begin to think creatively and outrageously about your living arrangements, full time, part time, and on your vacation. I wish you well.

Start by making a check list of what *is* important and what is *not* important to you.

Ruth Hoge, a woman past ninety, decided it was time she and her husband gave up the large house and garden. But they selected a condo that had a porch where she could grow plants. She also did some gardening on the grounds of her Quaker meeting. Grace Vicary went into a retirement community in Pennsylvania which meant giving up the town garden plot in Cambridge, Massachusetts, where those with apartments could have a bit of land to grow things. But she selected a retirement community in Pennsylvania that had gardens residents could cultivate. Whatever your priorities, there may be ways to accommodate them or adjustments that are worth changing your priorities.

One devotee of Elderhostels and travel decided that she didn't even want a home anymore. She put her savings into a very well appointed Recreational Vehicle and travels about the country to Elderhostels where she gets a special rate because, like a turtle, she carries her home with her. She has seen almost all the National Parks, makes friends in camping grounds, and often gets invited to come park her R.V. in people's driveways and explore their areas. You could do this kind of thing with a husband or friend if you are not a loner, though you make friends along the road.

I haven't gone completely turtle. I do have a house. But, being a writer,I know that I can go free or at very low cost to one of the artists' colonies around the country. There are more than 200 of these, subsidized by foundations and benefactors. So if you happen to be a composer, writer, artist, or other creative person, you might consider these as homes away from home. They usually offer communal meals and sociable evenings. You meet great people *and* get a lot of work done because you are away from the telephone and your relatives, friends, and other work or avocations. I have been to eight of them during the last decade for periods ranging from one to three months. One of these wonderful artists' colonies even offers a fellowship of free room and board for two months and an airplane ticket to get there for women who began to write seriously after age 55. This is the Frances Shaw Fellowship at the Ragdale Foundation, 1260 North Green Bay Road, Lake Forest, Illinois, 60045. The application deadline yearly is usually March 1. I have been at Ragdale, and found it comfortable, beautiful, and conducive to good work.

To find out about other colonies, you can buy a booklet, *Artist Colonies*, from The Center for Arts Information, 625 Broadway, New York, NY, 10012, or a larger book, *Grants and Awards Available to American Writers*, from the PEN American Center, 568 Broadway, New York, NY 10012. The magazine, *Poets & Writers*, also has information about these colonies and their deadlines. If this magazine is not in your library, you can subscribe: 72 Spring Street, New York, NY 10012. Don't be modest or think your work is not good enough. Think outrageously!

One very outrageous artist I know, doesn't even have a permanent home. She spends most of the year at various artists' colonies and stays with friends and relatives in between times. Her home is really at these colonies. Her post office address is the gallery which handles her paintings. The gallery owners forward her mail to her wherever she is.

Another person I know who has no home at all is a retired school teacher who spends May through September working for room and board as an evening desk clerk at a small inn in New England. During the cold months, she does the same thing at an inn in Florida.

This woman said that originally it was a wrench to get rid of all her possessions. She eased the pain by giving some to relatives and making a nice profit selling others. She uses her teacher's pension to support a comfortable lifestyle because in both her jobs she works only enough to earn her board and room. At sixty nine, she is delighted with the way she has worked things out. She says, "If I get tired of what I am doing, I'll think of something else. Meanwhile, I am saving money so I can afford something else some time." She has traded adventure for security—that is, she has decided her priority is to enjoy nice places rather than owning or renting a nice place.

Mary Plumley, a mid-sixty year old woman, has one of the most creative housing and lifestyle solutions I have seen. A widow, she fixed up a small but attractive apartment in the formerly unused basement at her daughter's New Hampshire home. But she lives there summers and during the Christmas/New Year period only. The rest of the year, she serves as volunteer conference director and Elderhostel coordinator at the Cook Theological School in Tempe, Arizona, a marvelous place, especially in contrast to New England winters. She gets free airfare from the school, a nice apartment, and her meals. She also has the satisfaction of knowing she is helping a school which trains Native Americans for the ministry and runs conferences for Native Americans.

Other volunteers, couples or individuals, who are retired also get away from cold weather by working at Cook. They serve as cooks, cleaners, gift shop staff. They, too, get living accommodations and free transportation. Some of them even run a thrift shop where clothes donated from churches all over the country can be bought for small sums by the Native Americans and their families who come to the Cook School to study or to attend conferences.

Mary finds the work challenging and meets fascinating Native Americans. I know a good deal about Mary and the Cook School because I, too, work there in February as an Elderhostel teacher. One year, Mary had a lot of trouble finding cooks. Some day, perhaps I will go out there for the whole winter and cook. There may be someplace like Cook, or Cook itself, where you could exchange services for being with others in a nice place.

There are more housing options than you can imagine. In this chapter, I have suggested some, but there are others which already exist or which you might invent. Put your creativity to this issue. Realize you do have options. As I have shown, not all of the options will cost you money. Some will even save you considerable money. And some may save you from being lonely.

For further research, Dr. Jane Porcino has an in-depth exploration of housing alternatives in her book *Living Longer, Living Better: Adventures in Community Housing for Those in the Second Half of Life*, Continuum Publishing Company, 370 Lexington Avenue, N.Y., N.Y., 10017, 1991.

CHAPTER NINE

Units of Belongingness

EVEN THOREAU left Walden. After his experiment in living in isolation, he went back to Concord to live near people. You may have decided you want to continue to live alone and like it. It affords you privacy and the freedom to do what you want when you want it. That is fine. Except for my forays to colonies and to youth and elderhostels, that is what I am doing. As a writer with peculiar hours and a noisy typewriter, I find living alone much of the time works well for me. But I have learned that units of belongingness are important for anyone, especially if you live alone or are aging and don't have the structure and interactions of daily work outside the home

In this chapter, I would like you to assess whether your units of belongingness are adequate and satisfactory and what new units you might develop. In the chapter on identity change, I suggested that affiliations of a new sort were important in supporting identity change. However, even if you are perfectly happy with your identity and want to keep it stable, you can enrich your life by having additional or better affiliations.

Families and friendships, to be covered in chapters ten and fourteen, are units of belongingness, but there are many others. A primary affiliation for many people is a religious affiliation which, besides providing spiritual sustenance, offers friendship and activities on a regular basis. A sixty-two year old woman who was feeling lonely, a live-alone, recently joined a busy church where there are activities she enjoys two or three nights a week. One night is choir rehearsal. A second night, she goes to a women's group at the church. Usually, on a third night a week there is a talk, a movie and discussion, or a committee meeting. These activities have made a big difference in her life.

When I got divorced, I found the religious grouping with which I had been affiliated was not very hospitable to fifty year old divorced women. I was quite welcome to come to services, but all activities, except for children and senior citizens, were basically for couples. I have tried several other congregations of this religion and found them similar. Once, I was even insulted by being told to bring a male friend to a social event, as if I were not good or sufficient enough to go as a woman alone. Another time, I became angry because a congregation had an ad for new members directed to couples without understanding that singles, too, might want or need to join.

Outrageous woman that I am, I complained about this ad to the clergyman who was insensitive enough to say that I was unduly sensitive and that in writing him a letter of complaint, I was "going after a gnat with a cannon." I have this man's letter in my files if you think I exaggerate.

Fortunately, there are other denominations and congregations that *do* have a place for single older women. And I found one. After being unaffiliated religiously for a number of years because of the Noah's Ark Syndrome, I found a denomination and a congregation in which I am most comfortable. I became a member of the Society of Friends, Quakers. My meeting has many single persons, mostly women since women predominate among the single and old. We also have couples and families who are non-discriminatory and very friendly to the singles. Belonging allows me to be with people of all statuses as a full status person, not a second class person.

I enjoy the women's group which is very supportive and meets one night a week. Ages there range from thirty to ninety-five. Equally enjoyable are the Friendly Eight groups where, once a month, eight people meet for a pot luck supper and a discussion on a topic of their choice. My Friendly Eight group has two single women, a married woman who comes without her husband who cares for the children that night, and three couples. So, actually, we are a Friendly Nine. Other groups are also a mixture of marital and non-marital status and age.

There are, of course, other activities including meeting for worship on Sunday, a monthly meeting for worship preceded by a pot luck supper, a yearly two day retreat which is great fun with the children, and assorted other activities.

This gives me a fine unit of belongingness and a group of people who are not necessarily close friends but upon whom I could call in an emergency and whom I can help in *their* emergencies. It was good, when one couple in the meeting had quadruplets, to be in a unit which provided meals for this family during the first hectic period. It was also good, when I had an auto accident, to have people from the meeting calling to see if they could do anything to help me, shop or provide transportation.

I am not trying to proselytize you for *my* religion, but simply to suggest that you might find a religious grouping that will help meet your needs. You may have to be outrageous, as I was, to make a change from the group where you have been affiliated, but, if it is not supportive, that may be necessary as you age.

If religion is not something you want in your life, there are many other routes to belongingness. Women's groups of all kinds exist all the way from political groups like the League of Women Voters to service clubs, women's support groups, professional and business women's groups, garden clubs, college alumni groups, groups organized around hobbies, etc. Most towns and cities list these in local newspapers. Chambers of Commerce or other such organizations often publish directories of clubs and organizations. Bulletin boards and local newspapers are good sources to find out which groups exist in your area. Don't be shy about going. Such groups are usually delighted with new recruits.

As mentioned in other chapters, volunteering is a good way to have a unit of belongingness if you no longer do paid work or do it only part time, or if you are a full time homemaker whose nurturees are gone. One of the fringe benefits of most volunteer jobs is that you are part of a group of volunteers who interact. My friend Ellie Mamber of Newton, who runs two volunteer programs (SHINE, which gives insurance information to elders, and a widows' program) brings her volunteers together once a month for an enjoyable meeting. She also arranges social events for them. The same is probably true of programs in your area.

The American Association of Retired Persons, with chapters

throughout the country, has frequent meetings, and, if you become really active, take an office, this can become a unit of belongingness.

Those who live in some close knit communities may belong to a neighborhood network, especially if someone in the neighborhood facilitates. An older couple I know hold a barbecue every Fourth of July for everyone on their street. This helps knit people together. Other neighbors have run neighborhood garage sales at a central location. Working together helps people to get to know one another. (It also moves junk from one house to another in the neighborhood since people are seduced by others' discards.)

But in many rural areas neighbors live at a distance, and in many urban ones people are not very neighborly. If this is your situation, you can either become a community builder or look elsewhere for belonging units.

Reading this may make you want to retch. You may have been a happy loner all your life or have enough friends so that your social needs are satisfied, and you don't need groups. That is fine. Congratulations on your choices which are good for you. The nagging in this chapter is not for you. It is for the older women who need to fill their calendars and their lives.

Some have already made common cause with other women by joining the local and national Older Women's League (OWL). (OWL National Office, 666 11th Street, N.W. Suite 700, Washington, D.C. 20001.) Others are so busy with responsibilities and commitments that what they need is some time and space for themselves. Being overorganized can fill you with rage because you have no time to nuture you. One woman said to me in harried voice, "I have to do something every night for the next two weeks. They are all good things to do and things I want to do, but I am tired just thinking about it." Yet, this same woman becomes anxious if her calendar is not filled. What she and other women need is a balance between being with others and being with one's self. It is hard to achieve this.

What makes the balance difficult is that many organizations, especially in areas that have bad winters or hot summers, schedule everything interesting in the few good months of the year. I have found that most of my invitations to speak are in October and April, the two best weather and holiday free months in New England. Many older women who live alone and look forward to events also find that peak months are too busy, and other months are empty. In the summer, there is very little going on in most places that are not resort areas. It is assumed people will be vacationing, and so little is scheduled. My group of Wellesley Friends decided to provide summer interaction by establishing Wellesley Wednesdays for the summer months. Each Wednesday, a fair number of people who stay around gather for a pot-luck supper and a discussion on some topic. Sometimes, one of us talks about a trip she has taken or shares an area of knowledge. It is informal, pleasant, and satisfying. Consider getting people together in your community to fill the hiatus of dull seasons.

Some suggestions for things to do with others have already appeared in the chapter on creative activities. In that chapter and this, I am seeking for you to rethink how you spend your time, who you spend it with, and how satisfactory or unsatisfactory this seems to you.

One of the exercises I often ask people to do in workshops is to divide a sheet of paper into three areas, list the things they enjoyed in their work outside or inside the home in younger days, the things they enjoyed doing with their family in younger days, and the things they enjoyed doing for themselves. Then, I ask them to consider what the *essence* of these activities were. For example, something you have enjoyed doing for yourself might be skiing. The essence of skiing is adventure, being outdoors, and being with others. Few people ski alone. The essence of cooking for a family might have been feeling creative and doing for others in a nurturing way. After people have identified the essence of what they liked to do in these three categories, I ask them to think about how they can capture that essence, now and at later ages. For example, the ski buff who can no longer ski can join a walking club or a bird club and have adventures, enjoy the outdoors, and be with others, achieving the essence of the former activity in a new way. The person who loved to nurture others by creative cooking and whose family has grown can now volunteer to cook in a soup kitchen or a shelter for battered women or the homeless. People have found this exercise useful. I hope you will try it.

In the course of it, if you are retired, you may find that what you miss about paid work is seeing people on a regular basis. Some people were not thrilled with the work itself but liked the interactions with people and going out to lunch with them Memberships in organizations may regularize your contact with people. Paid work gives us what I call the important "I's"—Interaction, Identity, Importance, Integrity, Interest, Income, and, one other important "I", Insurance. By insurance, I mean that people will know we are okay. One of the concerns of older women living alone is that, if they become ill or have a home accident, nobody will come to help. If people don't show up to paid work, someone eventually checks on them. In older years, when you do not have to be at work everyday, you need to make sure that someone will check on you. Some elders have gotten involved with formal organizations that provide such services, though some do it informally. One woman had an arrangement with her neighbor. If either of them did not raise windowshades in the morning by a certain time, the other would check on her with her key to her neighbor's house.

Tema Nason, a writer in the Boston area, conceived the idea of an organization of women who would agree to help each other out in case of illness by providing such services as driving each other to the doctor, picking up groceries or prescriptions, etc. There are informal ways, too, but also formal organized ways like Tema's for security and reciprocity. As government services are cut, older women may have to rely on families, friends, and each other for help. It is good to organize earlier rather than agonize later.

Independence and self reliance are great. We want to maximize these as long as possible. However, the aging process may mean some help is necessary. It is good to have a network for help as well as for sociability. Don't let shyness or pride stand in the way of getting your needs met.

Good luck in your search for units of belongingness and for units of support.

CHAPTER TEN

Be Outrageous
with Your Descendants

I SUGGEST that you begin to think of your children, grandchildren, and great grandchildren, if you are lucky enough to have them, as descendants, not as your children. Our language does not have a good word for adult offspring who are indeed no longer children. Thinking of these folks as your descendants may be the first step in freeing you from the idea that you are responsible for these adults. You did the best you could when your sons and daughters were children. Now they are responsible for themselves. Your grandchildren and great grandchildren are the responsibility of *their* parents, and you should not be telling these parents how to bring them up.

Women in our society are socialized to guilt. Mothers are the targets of all kinds of propaganda that makes them feel as if everything that happens to their descendants through life is their fault. That is just not true. In two parent families, fathers have responsibility too. Also, much of what happens to our children is the influence of the larger society through the schools, peer group, mass media, economy, historical period, and the state of the society. Women blame themselves unmercifully and erroneously for things that were never their faults.

Unfortunately, many adults are into mother-blaming. So we have a situation where older women are blaming themselves for imagined wrongs they did the children while adults who are dissatisfied with their lives are blaming their mothers and reinforcing the mother's guilt and misery. Some of my work is helping older mothers to eliminate this guilt, to help their descendants to stop using mother-blaming as a cop-out for their own lack of responsibility.

Our relationships with our adult daughters are especially important to us. They are more like us than our sons, and they are the caretakers if we are frail. It is very interesting, that, though we have been running public mother/daughter conferences through the Wellesley College Center for Research on Women for a dozen years, they are always over-subscribed. And we never seem to run out of topics. Indeed, the talk I prepared for one of the conferences became the best selling *Working Paper* of the Wellesley College Center for Research on Women precisely because so many women find the relationship difficult. Here is what the paper said.

MOTHERS, DAUGHTERS, GRANDMOTHERS, GRANDDAUGHTERS

Generations

I once briefly a daughter
now always a daughter
dream of daughter
she is the mirror
in which I see
my mother's eyes
look back at me.

Women are linked through the generations, but we do not know a great deal about those linkages. Although culture and life itself have been transmitted through women, the public sphere has been more researched and valued than lineal relationships. The lives of men and the influence of men on women have generally been considered more important than the lives of women and women's contributions.

In the last few years, there have been several books and articles and a number of conferences on the topic of mothers and daughters. In many of these, the tension between mothers and daughters has been emphasized, and some reconciliation has been sought.

I would like to continue this exploration by pointing out some of the dilemmas that mothers, daughters, grandmothers, and grand-daughters face in their relationships and relate these dilemmas to the contemporary American context in which the roles are enacted.

However, a feminist always questions the biases of anyone, including herself, so I must start by exposing mine: First is my professional stance. I am a sociologist and tend to see individual thought and behavior as reflecting social structures.

Second is my personal situation. As my starting poem said, I was only *briefly* a daughter. My mother died when I was ten, and the rest of mothering came from aunts, a grandmother, a stepmother for less than a year, teachers, and women of various sorts. Perhaps most influential was my grandmother, and I tell about her in a poem. To understand this, you need to know that Ellis Island was where European immigrants were processed in the early twentieth century.

Grandmother

My grandmother, Marmita
was given the name Minnie
at Ellis Island
and carefully traced it
on the report cards
of five children.
It was all the English
she could ever write.

When her oldest child
my mother, died at thirty
she took a ten year old
and a three year old
and traced Minnie
on our report cards
and on all those forms
to get legal guardianship
and state aid to feed us.

She crocheted doilies
for the social worker
begged clothes and camps
and within a slum
kept a shining house.

Half crazed
by her daughter's death
and endless poverty
she cried, screamed,
had no patience
with my brother
and even threatened me
good, too good, though I was.

But every spring
somewhere in that slum
she stole lilacs
to put upon my dresser
and trace her love
forever on me.

As mentioned earlier, I was also helped by many other women. This is often true of those who were undermothered for reasons other than maternal death. Both men and women in our society sometimes spend a lifetime seeking nurturance and being bitterly disappointed when it is not forthcoming. Therapists of both sexes often become paid nurturers, but most is expected of women therapists, educators, neighbors, or friends. Here is a poem I call

Lifelong

The motherless
have many
mothers.
Each woman's

pregnant face
invites
seduction
rejection
always.

It is very important to understand that despite the contrary and often sexist literature – psychoanalytical and otherwise – it is not the failure of mothers that leaves people hungry for nurturance or hostile to mothers. Our society is anti-nurturant, and even cruel, on the whole, and people do not usually get their human needs met in schools, in the workplace, or even in our troubled marriages. It is no surprise that there is an inordinate and unrealistic expectation that mothers supply endlessly the warmth and help that is otherwise generally lacking. Mothers are also a relatively safe target.

Sometimes, we who are middle-aged and older women wonder why our daughters and sons continue to pull at us or fault us now for old or new sins even though we gave them our best when they were young and still do so. The answer is, I think, that the world as it is today gives them very little, and they turn their rage on those who gave them the most and who are accepting of them. It is also easier to blame one's mother than one's self or an impersonal society.

Perhaps the most hostile and unreconciled of all our sons and daughters are those who were adolescents and young adults in the sixties. That generation's youth was marked by a social climate in which there were great hopes of restructuring society in a more humane way. Those who have utopian dreams dashed are all the more bitter than those who have low expectations.

Mothers become the scapegoats not only for children but, in fact, for the entire society. As I wrote in my book *Life After Youth: Female, Forty, What Next?* (Beacon Press, Boston, 1979), we women make the mistake of thinking this angry undercurrent of offspring and society toward older women is our fault instead of seeing its true cause in the larger society's failure and scapegoating. Actually, we gave our sons and daughters and society a great deal, but we could not make up for the fact that males generally make poor fathers because of the stresses on them, and that other social institutions are troubled.

Even though my mother died when I was ten, she gave me, personally, enough to make a life on. Because she read to me and took me to parks though we were urban poor, I became a writer and a lover of nature. I would like to share with you a poem telling what I got from my mother and other mother surrogates in my life.

Maternal Heritage

From my mother
the love of poems
and violets
from my grandmother
giving when
there is little
left to give
from one aunt
an artist's eye
and from another
courage despite
recurrent tragedy
from a near-mother
competence at work
and from still
another nurturer
keeping compassion
within the bounds
of self-respect.

As there have been many mothers in my life, there have also been many daughters. I have one marvelous blood daughter, Edith Jane, who is now thirty-five and a rehabilitation worker. (I also have a son, Eliha.) But I have many additional daughters in the women who have been my students since I started teaching college in 1968 after getting a late education ending with a Ph.D. at forty-five. Because women faculty are a scarce resource, I mother many women students.

Incidentally, these young women, when confiding in me, often say, "If I could only talk to my own mother the way I do to you." I have to reply that if I were their own mothers, they could not talk to me as freely, because of that fact. Students are at an age when, to mature and fit into a mobile society, they must individuate and claim their independence from the very person who is really most dear, though often seemingly rejected. This fact brings me to the first dilemma that mothers and daughters face.

Dilemma one: As daughters must often painfully become independent from their mothers, the mothers must also often painfully give up a role which has been a prime gratification. There is relief as well as loss, of course. Though most women work outside the home now, many who are older were full-time homemakers and invested heavily in the one role, mothering, for which they got social approval and personal gratification, along with some troubles. They must give up the role in a society which often, as I documented in *Life After Youth*, gives women few good options later in life.

The loss of the mothering role sometimes coincides, for the woman, with the loss of wifehood because men die on the average eight years younger and marry women considerably younger than themselves. In addition, today, divorce among older marriages is common and, though the men can remarry readily, it is harder for women to have late-in-life male partners because there are fewer men in these age groups and because the available men usually prefer much younger women.

The older woman who seeks nurturant work as fulfillment, or because she is a displaced homemaker, generally finds this work is in short supply even if she has the credentials. We are cutting down on human services in the society. So the older woman must give up a special relationship with her children just at a time when there are few other opportunities to continue the accustomed nurturance.

A second dilemma for these women is that this society devalues older people in general, but especially older women. Thus, the very maturity of her daughter reminds the mother that she is aging and must suffer the social consequences of this. Her joy at her daughter's womanhood is tempered by her own loss of social esteem in a society with a double standard of aging. Though she might like to live through her daughter, this is something few mothers can or should do, and certainly something few daughters can permit.

For the daughter, the dilemma is that she sees the unhappiness society inflicts on her aging mother and vows never to become like her, but secretly fears she may. Thus, to reject a feared fate, she rejects the mother and blames the mother for being unhappy. The daughter is frequently unable to see or acknowledge that the mother is a societal casualty. This is because, if the daughter acknowledges the mother's victimhood, she must be conscious that she too could become a victim. Acknowledging this possibility might produce not only fear but also the necessity for militancy and advocacy – attitudes which are not popular and are, indeed, often ridiculed or punished, by males in particular and by society in general.

The tragedy is that in denying their mothers, younger women often deny reality and their own aging. They lose the opportunity to learn how to prepare for their own older womanhood. And, of course, they hurt their mothers dreadfully. Besides this, women who should be allies are separated into the young and the old.

A third dilemma is that the daughters' and mothers' values are often very different. There has been a marked change in sexual norms and behavior as well as in women's roles in general. The mother may applaud the new morés and wish they had existed in her youth, feeling gypped. A woman socialized in another era may be accepting of the daughter's values and behavior or may reject them outright, or be ambivalent. Even if a mother is accepting, she may realistically or unrealistically be afraid that her daughter will be hurt. On her side, the daughter may suffer conflict between the values of the peer group and those of the mother and be resentful. She may also be resentful about the mother's anxiety for another reason: If the daughter is coping with, or denying, her own ambivalence or anxiety, it may become more difficult if her mother's anxiety is a constant reminder of the problematic nature of life for women in a violent, sexist society.

A fourth dilemma is that many daughters today have elected to remain unmarried or childless. This deprives the mother of grandmotherhood, which might provide some reaffirmation of her generativity and immortality through the bloodline. Now, grandmotherhood in modern society is hardly a full-time role in most cases. Indeed, it is often pretty marginal in our society, with our grandmothers often employed or at a distance geographically or emotionally for various reasons. Nevertheless, it is hard for the woman who would like grandchildren if they are not forthcoming. She feels especially deprived and even feels a sense of failure if her daughter, rather than her son, does not reproduce. Still, she must respect her daughter's choice and refrain from criticism or prodding if the relationship is not to be injured. The daughter, in her turn, must control her resentment if the mother pushes for what the daughter does not desire. If there are grandchildren, there are, of course, often dilemmas around their raising too obvious to discuss here.

As one who does not myself have grandchildren, I would suggest that there are other ways of being in contact with new generations than through official grandmotherhood. There are many volunteer programs in which one can work with needy girls. Girls in juvenile justice systems are greatly at risk and need help. Have you visited your local detention center lately? Young girls are often held in horrible circumstances for long periods for such status offenses as running away from home. Many have run from abuse and incest.

There are also constant informal ways of being a nurturer as I wrote in a poem called

Generativity

I lust for the ocean.
In May when sunners huddle
shawls on the beach
I swim the waves alone
warm with joy.
In Harwich Port
my ownership was challenged
when Liz, seven and a half,
introduced herself
by asking how I floated.
"Don't be afraid
and you won't sink."
She replied, "I'll play dead."

"Never dead," I told her
"Just relax—the water holds."
Neither of us cold,
fifty swam with seven
I taught her how to float
while her parents sunned
and Liz stroked my toes
in gratitude, teaching love.
I am Ruth
and wherever you go, Liz
I shall go
In the spring you are fifty
you will recall
how a May swimmer
taught you courage.
Though I shall be long gone,
I will live then in you
my sister and my child
of the year's first ocean swim.

What I tried to say in that poem is that we can touch youngsters with our generativity, and this provides gratification and immortality also. Perhaps, then, it is easier to release our own children.

Another dilemma of the mother-daughter role occurs when the mother is aged if she is frail. Then, the daughter is often called upon to do for the mother. It is hard for both when dependency becomes reversed.

I was asked once, to speak at the Scarsdale, New York, Adult School about the relations that the middle generation has with aging parents and also with nearly grown or grown-up children. I started to devise some suggestions for each situation and suddenly realized that the guidelines were the same for dealing with both generations. Actually, though, it is largely women who are the kin keepers and who do most of the relationship work in families. So I would like to share my rules here, though they have been printed in *Dynamic Years* magazine, July–August 1981.

For mothers, daughters, grandmothers, granddaughters:

* Never do *anything* for them that they can do for themselves. This infantilizes and creates dependency and anger.
* Never make plans for them without consulting them. Practically everyone functions better with a sense of autonomy and options.
* Avoid the utopianization of youth or old age. You cannot make things perfect for your children or your parents.
* Never shortchange yourself or postpone your own living. Do not be callous, but do respect your needs. Otherwise, you will become resentful, and it will show and poison relationships.
* Know and use outside resources. There are community programs and good advisers for both young and old.
* Get support from mid-lifers in the same boat. You are not alone. Do not re-invent the wheel.
* Save something for your old age. You do not have to sacrifice yourself to the generations behind and ahead.
* Be honest. Both young and old people would rather have the truth than evasiveness. You cannot fool either.
* Be patient with both. Youth and old age are stressful in American society, and both young and old are grasping for status in a society which devalues them.
* Do not talk down to either generation. Be yourself. Do not reach for the current slang to communicate with the young, and avoid talking geri-talk (demeaning simplification) to the old. In other words, respect the ability of the young and the old.
* Try to laugh with both, but not at them. Shared laughter bonds. Mockery wounds.

I have only just begun to list dilemmas between mothers and daughters. There is much more to talk about and think about and correct. What is most important, however, is to go beyond the dilemmas. There is too much negativity everywhere and even in these comments ascribed to a relationship that has many positive aspects. In fact, the mother-daughter-grandmother-great grandmother linkage has been greatly underestimated in terms of its contributions to our lives and our culture. We have received more than we know.

It is really good to think out what you want from and for your adult daughter at this point in your lives. I did this two years ago, writing for our Mother/Daughter day a poem, the longest I have ever written, setting forth what I think are the thoughts of many old mothers. It follows:

1.

We old mothers want for our daughters
granddaughters and great granddaughters
what every woman has a right to expect
and what so few really, ultimately have.
We want daughters to live in a world
where all women are valued in youth
middle age and old age whatever their
physical attributes, health or preference,
where women are safe in streets and homes
and have respected work, growth and love
without war between peoples and genders.

2.

In our old age, we review our lives
and our seemingly senseless society.
We have moments of terror, knowing
we leave our beloved daughters a world
which still considers them unequal,
"cunts," cheap labor, burden bearers,
nurturers to children, men and society
but not to themselves without censure,
targets of mockery, lust and violence,
expendable scapegoats for that alienation
pervading, polluting, poisoning people.

3.

As old mothers, we ask ourselves
could we better have prepared
our daughters for an uncaring world?
What could we have taught, modeled
to arm, cushion, support, guide,
comfort, show daughters the way, now

or when we can no longer help,
need help ourselves, or are gone?
Who will be there for our daughters
when they have no mothers?
Please, will there be others?

4.

Meanwhile, some of us are grateful
that our daughters value us
extend transgenerational friendship.
Their love lights our later years.
Others of us suffer deeply from
daughters' misfortunes or flaws.
When unhappy daughters condemn
overtly or in silence, we agree.
Our society teaches women guilt
so we blame ourselves, not fate
or the difficulties of living.

5.

Having little power in the world,
we sought omnipotent motherhood
to make all happy, make no mistakes,
be perfect in an imperfect world.
We despair if our daughters continue
to nurse old hurts, refuse to grow,
are stuck in mother-blaming,
easier, safer than blaming selves
or accepting an unfair, cold world.
Some daughters even fault mothers
for aging which mirrors their futures.

6.

Rejected mothers want from daughters
reconciliation, empathy, even thanks
but are too proud to plead or if they do
are called all the more destructive.
Can they accept that the upbringing

was shared with fathers, schools, society?
Even the daughters themselves had volition.
Can such daughters express their rage
against those real hurts and enemies
which injured both their mothers,
themselves and still sadly persist?

7.

Also can mothers realize we survived
our tragedies and most daughters will too?
We gave them more than we now know
or than daughters or men can know.
Mistakes were made in love and ignorance.
We can still use our last strength, courage
and crones' wisdom to strive with daughters
for a world that accords all persons
compassion, control, creativity and hope.
Can all ages of women, ceasing quarrels
unite with understanding of our common work?

After I wrote this poem, Janet Putnam, assistant director of the
Wellesley Center raised the question "what do daughters of old mothers want for the mothers?" I asked some younger women and then
wrote my estimation of what they might want, calling this poem

We Daughters of Old Mothers

We daughters want for our mothers
what they so often do not receive –
respect for the fullness of their years
instead of denigration for their aging.
We want them to be treated as humans
not as disabilities or nuisances.
We want their wisdom and talents
to be fostered, flowered and valued.

If our mothers are infirm and needy
we want society to which they gave freely
to reciprocate respect and compassionate care
not the current rationing of resources
or the making of daughters sole caregivers—
a burden aging daughters should not carry.
As daughters, we do not want to fear
that we will become resentful, drained.
We want sufficient, decent social services.

We want our mothers to live out their years
in dignity whatever their circumstances.
We do not want them to be reminders of how
we might someday be neglected or humiliated.
We want our relationships with our mothers
to be loving in sickness as well as in health
but there are limits to what we can do alone.
Many of us also have husbands, descendants,
jobs and even needs of our own to meet.

Like our mothers, we would like to resolve
old hurts, misunderstandings, deprivations.
We seek the wisdom and perspective to know
that our mothers too experienced social injury
and hurt us because they were hurt and isolated.
Before they leave this world, we want to say
"we understand your human limitations, weakness,
as we understand and respect our own."

In forgiving old mothers, we forgive ourselves.
In loving old mothers, we will love ourselves.
In working for social justice for our mothers
we will work for our own entitlement some day
and for the welfare of our blood daughters
or any daughters of this society and planet.

Why Older Mothers Have a Tough Time

If we are concerned, we are overprotective;
    if we are unconcerned, we are neglectful.
If we nurture generously, we are smothering;
    if we nurture less, we are withholding.
If we are successful, we are intimidating;
    if we are unsuccessful, we are poor role models.
If we are available, we encourage dependency;
    if we are busy ourselves, we are detached.
If we offer advice, we are controlling;
    if we refrain, we are disinterested.
If we phone, write or visit often, we are pests;
    if we don't, we are thought uncaring.
If we give or loan money, we engender resentment;
    if we don't give or loan money, we are cheap.
If we help with their tasks, we are drudges;
    if we don't, we are considered lazy.
If we love husbands or others best, we put them first;
    if we love descendants first, we have no life of our own.
If we put ourselves last, we have no self love;
    if we put ourselves first, we are narcissistic.
If we hide our needs, we are martyrs;
    if we reveal our needs, we are demanding.
If we provide for our old age, we are selfish;
    if we don't provide, we are burdens.
If we pitch in, we question their competency;
    if we don't pitch in, they question our competency.

If all or some of this is true, we might as well
    do what we wish and do it OUTRAGEOUSLY.

CHAPTER ELEVEN

Sexuality

SEXUALITY in later life is such an important topic that, besides giving you some information in this chapter, I am going to provide, at the end of it, a bibliography so you can do further reading. But I hope reading is not all you will be able to do about your sexuality. For *Older Women Surviving and Thriving*, I was going to write a few vignettes about various ways older women could express their sexuality. However, I found that there were so many ways that I had to write an alphabet from Anne to Zena. When I got to Zena, I was sorry there were only twenty-six letters in the alphabet because I could go on writing variations. (See the end of this chapter for the alphabet.)

Just after that book was published, I spoke at a National Association of Social Workers Massachusetts meeting at Boston University, and some of the social workers went into shock when I read this alphabet. A number even went into shock at Anne and Barbara and never heard the rest of the alphabet.

I didn't think it was so shocking what I wrote about Anne and Barbara:

ANNE who is married has sexual intercourse with her husband though not quite as frequently as in younger years. The pleasure is excellent. Anne and her husband have longer foreplay than they used to because it takes him longer to get an erection, and they sometimes have oral sex which works well. They have also gotten some information from their doctor about positions and techniques which are more comfortable for older people. Among these are that Anne stimulates her husband's genitals with her caresses and he stimulates her and that they use a sideways position.

117

Anne also uses K-Y jelly as a clitoral and vaginal lubricant although her friend, Sara, uses a prescription item her doctor recommended.

BARBARA who is single has a male friend who generally spends one night a week at her apartment and shares her bed. She has known him for several years, having met him at the senior center shortly after his wife died. Sometimes they vacation together.

After the meeting many social workers thanked me for my courage in discussing older women's sexuality frankly. The responses of the shocked social workers, and the congratulatory ones, amazed and saddened me. Social workers are well educated, mostly women, and one would think that they would be accepting of older women's sexuality, not fazed by hearing it discussed. After that meeting, I started to do workshops on older women's sexuality because I realized that ageism meant that older women were supposed not to be sexual or were supposed to keep their sexuality in the closet. To simplify things, I wrote the following piece of doggerel which gives the story quickly.

Sex after sixty
can be nifty
and quite thrifty
unless you're shifty
the kind of louse
who cheats on spouse
and dies of fear
that spouse will hear.

When you're old
variations unfold
you like as well
with no alarm bell.
In later years
no need for tears
that he's too quick
or she's morning sick.

Aging sex is pleasure
quite a treasure
alone or with a mate

unless you hate
your sexuality
consider it triviality
have side effects
from medical treks
or worry so much
you don't dare touch
for fear of failure.
Old age sex, we hail ya.

Obviously, older sexuality is not quite as simple as that verse implies. In the rest of this chapter, I will deal with some of the complexities.

Sexuality is much more than mechanics. Sexuality has to do with our humanity as people who love and express our love in a sensual embrace of others and selves. Ideally, intercourse is a paradigm of human reciprocity, but sexuality is much broader than genital intercourse. Barbara F. Turner and Catherine Adams state: "Sexuality refers primarily to sexual behaviors and fantasies. In research on older people, behaviors typically studied are heterosexual intercourse and frequency of orgasm: less often, frequency of masturbation, homosexual contacts, kissing and fondling, and attitudes like interest in sex have been assessed. As several writers have pointed out, researchers have tended to focus on frequency counts and underemphasized the emotional context of sexuality, despite the importance of this facet of sexuality to most women (and men). More generally, sexuality refers to any sensual experience that has erotic overtones for a particular individual and also to those aspects of interactions with others that affirm a person's sense of femininity or masculinity." (*Older Women*, page 55, edited by Elizabeth W. Markson, Lexington Books, Lexington, MA, 1983.)

The truth is that most people are sexual all their lives, actively or in the broader sense that includes sensuality, intimacy needs, and interest. Behavior reflects opportunity or lack of partners, preferences, and many other factors. The varieties of sexual experience and interest are even more varied than Anne to Zena because humans and their circumstances are so varied. In the foreign film, *My Life as a Dog*, a dying elderly man asks a young boy to read to him a catalogue advertising women's underwear. Interests persist when physical expression cannot. However, activity does persist for a large percentage of people through all of life. Men who have, at older ages, long abstinence may become impotent but women do not lose capacity though the first intercourse after abstinence may be painful and lubricants required.

Yet we are a society that sees only youth as beautiful and sexually desirable, especially in the case of women. Many young people think old people are asexual or that sex would degrade elders, being perverse after youth. This is wrong. Older people have the same needs and right to sex as anyone. Older women are particularly seen as mother or grand-mother figures who ought to be chaste and Madonna-like. (Many people transfer feelings about their parents or grandparents, left over from childhood or adolescence when they dared not consider their parents, and especially their mothers, sexual.)

Other people think that when we are old, we become too fragile for sex, that it might hurt us. Generally, that is not so. Studies of coronaries during intercourse show that only one percent of such heart attacks occur during intercourse and that is, as I said in the doggerel earlier in this chapter, often in the case of illicit intercourse when the anxiety factor adds to the exercise. The exercise of sexual intercourse is about equivalent to climbing a flight of stairs.

Caretakers, such as physicians, also transfer to patients attitudes toward parents. Women have died unnecessarily of uterine cancer because their doctors failed to do pelvic examinations after a certain age. The mother of a dear friend went to several doctors complaining of "a hellish burning down there" and the doctor told her it was normal to have dryness in old age and not to worry about it. It is normal to have vaginal dryness in old age and lubricants are useful, but the hellish burning turned out to be connected with uterine cancer in her case. By the time it was diagnosed, it was too late for corrective measures. A pelvic exam including PAP smear should have been utilized for this eighty year old even if she did look like the doctors' grandmothers.

Those physicians who are inhibited about the sexuality of older patients, especially women, are not much use to them in counselling or in providing needed information which is why you should, if you have need, dip into the reading list I have provided.

As some of these books point out, especially those of Robert

Butler, M.D., some sexual dysfunction or impotence is related not to the process of aging or illness but rather is the result of the side effects of medications. Patients are often too inhibited to ask physicians about alternative medications that would not have this side effect. Even sophisticated patients are ignorant in this area, and their doctors fail to inform them.

Not only does male impotence result from certain prescriptions, female lack of libido can also. In one of my workshops, a highly educated woman in her late fifties said that her relationship with her husband was adversely affected by the fact that she was now disinterested in sex and could not be sexually aroused. Before getting into fancy reasons, I asked first what medications she was taking. It turned out that for four years she had been taking a tranquilizer that has a libido diminishing reaction. As we explored, we discovered that her sexual disinclination began shortly after she started to take this drug, and she had never made the connection. She should probably not have been on that tranquilizer anyway for four years.

You should ask your physician about the side effects of drugs. Then you and the doctor can discuss your willingness or unwillingness to experience them. Drugs can react differently in older people than younger ones. Not all physicians are skilled in adjusting medications for age. Some older persons have found useful the book *Worst Pills: Best Pills*: the older adult's guide to avoiding drug induced death or illness, prepared by Sidney M. Wolfe, M.D. and colleagues for the Public Health Research Group in 1988, and available for $12 from Pills, 2000 P Street, N.W. Suite 700, Washington, D.C. 20036. This book, of course, deals with other reactions to medication in addition to sexual dysfunction.

In regard to sexual activity, it is important to understand that people who have not been very active sexually or focused on sexuality in younger years are not suddenly going to become sexual athletes in later life. You may have not been enthusiastic earlier. Then you are not likely to be so now. Many lifelong celibates have productive happy lives, and you should not think yourself abnormal if you are content in your later years without overt sexual activity. You may enjoy other sensual aspects of life and express love friendship in non-sexual or sublimated ways.

Knowing the shortage of men in their age brackets and being committed only to heterosexual sex, many older women live out their lives getting other kinds of gratification or accepting sexual deprivation. There are over two million widowers and over eleven million widows beyond the age of 65. Many of those widowers will date, mate, or marry younger women. Divorced and widowed men re-marry much quicker and more often than women. With the gender imbalance, it is a male buyer's market, and there is a double standard of aging. Older women can sometimes re-marry, and some yearn for tips on meeting men. However, when Barbara H. Vinick, Ph.D., and I did a study of re-married couples past sixty, we found that the men were much more eager to remarry than the women. (See *Re-engagement in Later Life: Re-employment and Re-Marriage*, Ruth H. Jacobs and Barbara H. Vinick, Greylock Press, Stamford, Conn. 1979.) Many women enjoyed being free and responsible only for themselves.

The research shows that older men without partners who are socially sanctioned have about the same level of sexual activity as those who are married, but that older women without socially sanctioned partners have less activity. Despite the sexual revolution, older women often feel it necessary to have commitment. Here is an example of the different values of certain older men and women in statements made by Elderhostel participants that I fictionalized to disguise identities. This originally appeared in my book *Out of Their Mouths* (American Studies Press, Tampa, Florida, 1988).

PHILIP

I am Philip, a widower for seven years.
I hope I meet a nice woman here who
would like a real relationship if you know
what I mean.
There are a lot of women around because they
live longer than men but they are unwilling
to be close.
Sure I am interested in a permanent
relationship but how could I know if it is
someone I could be compatible with if we

don't get intimate?
Besides, I like to touch.
Women are so afraid to touch.
I like women who keep themselves young.
Just because you are old, you don't have to
look it. You can color your hair.
I do. I take a lot of pains to keep myself
looking young.
I don't like to say how old I am but if you
promise not to tell anyone, I'll tell you.
I am seventy-two.
Aren't you surprised?

CAROLINE

I am Caroline and I am only 65.
I resent very much what Philip just said
about women.
We aren't cold but women of my generation
don't want to be intimate without
commitment first.
Philip, you'd better try young women of the
now generation like the one I overheard at
an AIDS meeting who said, "I couldn't ask
him to use a condom; I hardly knew him."
In my day, you didn't even kiss until you
really knew someone.
Philip, another reason women don't jump at
you is they nursed one man through a final
illness and they don't want to take you on.
You do look 72; I am not surprised.
As for me, I am willing at 65 to wear grey
hair and admit that I am old.

Not all women, though, are like Caroline. One woman, we will call
her Marcia, was divorced at sixty and did not like the single life. She
told me she was determined to be re-married by the time she was

sixty-five. She was. This woman really worked at meeting men. She answered and put personal ads in magazines and newspapers that carry such ads, joined Single Booklovers, an organization that matches singles by their reading and other interests, and joined a computer dating service that arranged matches. She also let all friends and relatives know that she was looking for a husband. She dated and mated a number of men and did not seem to be terrified by fears of venereal disease. This was a few years ago before AIDS was as widespread and spreading to the general population rather than simply being confined to high risk categories. Marcia also felt she did not have to worry about being hurt, raped, or robbed by men she met through ads because she screened them on the telephone, then met them the first few times in restaurants in busy areas. She did not give her address to the men or let them come to her home until she was sure they were safe and she liked them.

When Marcia found a man she liked who reciprocated her affection, she went on several vacations with him and spent many weekends with him to try things out before they were married. He was seven years older, but she considered this acceptable. For her, the search was productive, and she has been happily married for two years now.

Some women who would like to be re-married or have a steady relationship are not willing to work at it the way Marcia did. Not all who do work at it are lucky enough to find a man willing to settle down. A 65 year old managed through a friend's introduction to meet a man who spends every weekend with her, but he is not interested in re-marriage.

Married women and women who aspire to marriage or sexual relationships with dates at older ages, need to know some facts about male sexuality. Older men often need more arousal time and more physical stimulation to be aroused. Some physical techniques with which an older woman can arouse her partner are explained in the sexuality chapter of the book *Ourselves Growing Older*, in the booklist at the end of this chapter. It is also important that the woman not increase a man's anxiety because anxiety itself can contribute to impotence. Widowers sometimes have psychological blocks, feeling disloyal to the dead wife, or prolonged abstinence may make difficulties.

At older ages, men have less of a need to ejaculate, but there is a plus to this in that men can make love and satisfy partners longer. They also have a lifetime of experience. There are some changes in women after menopause including dryness and the fact that the uterus may not elevate as much, creating less room for the vagina to expand and accommodate the penis. Hormone therapy is a controversial treatment for the dryness. You need to discuss this with a competent physician who knows your history. K-Y jelly is useful for dryness.

Don't think you are no longer desirable or a male is disinterested if, at older ages, he does not make love as frequently or it takes longer to get an erection. You need to understand his physiological changes as well as your own. Many older couples get pleasure out of being together and physical pleasuring such as massage. Sometimes good counselling by professionals can be very helpful, as can changes in medication, timing, positions, and techniques.

Some older women who have no partners or prospects self stimulate or pleasure themselves. Others do not have this outlet or feel guilty about it because of childhood and religious prohibitions. Once, when doing an Older Women's Surviving and Thriving Workshop, I asked the women participating to write anonymously how they expressed their sexuality. The women were from fifty to eighty. Some wrote about partners and some about deprivation but more than half of the thirty women wrote about the joys of self pleasuring, with or without lubricants, candlelight, and fantasies.

You may wonder why I have not used the word masturbation. It is because this term, as Edith Hamilton has pointed out, comes from the Latin meaning to pollute with the hand and has thus negative connotations left over from a more prudish era.

Other older women have, in the absence of male partners or out of a preference long suppressed, chosen to love women in their later years. Some express this in overt and complete sexual relationships and others in sublimated forms. Life long lesbians have the same deprivations as heterosexual women when their partners predecease them. They also suffer a great deal because legalities may mean that estates, including homes, go to distant relatives rather than to the lover if there is no strong will. Older lesbians are often discriminated against when they suffer the pain of the loss of a lover. In one town, an older lesbian tried to join a widows' group to help with her grieving and was badly treated by some of the widows. She left the group even though the leader was supportive of her.

In married heterosexual couples, it can be tragic if one member believes he or she is done with sex or wants to be done with it, and the other is still interested. Once, after a workshop I gave on sexuality, a woman midlifer called for my help with her parents. It seemed her father, near eighty, still wanted intercourse but his wife did not. This daughter asked me if I knew of a nice clean surrogate I could recommend for her father who was very disgruntled.

I am not outrageous enough to have a list of surrogates or prostitutes and thought it a bit strange that a daughter would offer that solution. I pointed out to the daughter a number of things to consider. I will repeat them here.

1. The mother might have some physical condition such as dryness or lesions which might make intercourse painful, and the help of a caring, good gynecologist might be enlisted.

2. The father might have been a poor lover through a lifetime so that the mother disliked their sex life. She might consider herself entitled to be retired by reason of age from a distasteful experience.

3. The father might be careless about his cleanliness and be offensive.

4. The father, at this late date, might need some instruction in how to make the sex act pleasurable for his partner.

5. There might be things going on out of bed in this couple's life that meant the woman was angry at her husband. Maybe incompatibility on other matters is beneath the mother's sexual aversion. If the couple were not getting along well in non-sexual life, it would be no surprise that their sexual life was undermined. These problems might be addressed by good couple or individual counselling. It is not too late at any age to get help.

6. There might be medication that was decreasing or eliminating the mother's libido.

7. The mother might have internalized the sexual ageism in society and made up her mind that sex was not appropriate at her age. In that case, she could read the sexuality chapter in *Ourselves Growing Older*, the Butler book, or other books or articles on the topic. She could

find out that non-sexuality in the old is a myth and she could also learn some techniques.

8. There might have been other factors such as poor nutrition or depression that could be addressed to change her attitudes and mood. The physical and emotional are tied together. Even exhaustion can create sexual disinterest. The mother could be anemic or have another condition or might be overworking and not getting any help with household chores from a retired husband expecting three meals a day and maid service.

Of course, the more common scenario is when the wife is still interested and the male is having the impotency problems discussed earlier. The videotape at the end of this chapter (*Aging & Sexuality* from the University of Nebraska) has very specific information on how to help male impotence by various ways including implants. Many older couples do not know implants are available. They fail to ask their physicians about them, and physicians don't usually inquire about this aspect of life.

Implants which make intercourse possible may be displeasing to some couples, but others may welcome them gracefully. Whatever the sexual arrangements of older couples, they need to be pleasing to both partners. As in younger years, people need to be understanding, informed, and flexible.

Some women are sexually and socially inhibited in later years because of slight or serious urinary incontinence. It is important that older women do their Kegal exercises which are described in the *Ourselves Growing Older* book and in other places. These improve the grip of the vagina and are useful sexually but also help with urinary continence. Do not allow yourself to be socially isolated if you have an incontinence problem that good help from physicians cannot cure. Much incontinence can be cured. Experiment with the many products now on the market to control the moisture, and realize that there are many others our age with the same problem.

I have a problem only when I have a bad cold and cough or sneeze hard. During those brief periods, I wear those glue-on panty shields in the super size that menstruating young women wear. We can take advantage of the new technology developed since we were menstruating and had to wear sanitary belts and cumbersome pads. New super pads are lightweight and odor absorbing. I mention this because it is usually a taboo subject. In my workshops, when I ask women to write their problems anonymously, I have found that leakage is frequently mentioned. It is no disgrace. It can be managed.

If you are a woman alone who is not pleased by any of the suggestions in this chapter but still feel angry because you have no partner, I have advice for you. Give to yourself in other ways. We can accept one kind of deprivation if we are not deprived in other ways. Give yourself presents instead of giving them to others. Go to the best restaurants you can afford and luxuriate in them instead of always eating cheap junk food because that is all you think you are worth. Give yourself sensual experiences other than sex. Swim, which is so sensual they might ban it if they knew. Join a health club and get your body massaged by the whirlpool, or by the masseuse if you can afford it. Wear soft fabrics and rub lovely smelling lotions onto your body. I will never forget seeing one beautiful seventy-five year old woman at my indoor swimming pool singing to herself as she stood naked in our dressing room rubbing nice lotion all over herself. She was cherishing her body and not ashamed of it. I also remember, at a retreat center, going into whirlpools into which fragrant flowers had been thrown to release a heavenly perfume. We were all undressed. Some of us had mastectomy scars, and others of us had bags of fat in various places, wrinkles or other imperfections, but we were all enjoying our bodies and not ashamed to have others see them. It was a liberating experience for me who had been body shy before this.

If sex is not an option for you now, there are other ways to enjoy physical beauty. Buy cheap paints, or good paints if you can afford them, and start painting. Dance alone to music if you must dance alone, but dance. Touch children, friends, in non-sexual ways. Handshakes and hugs can be nice. Many older women tell me that nobody ever touches them. That is a loss because we are beings who need touch. In my workshops, I have women get up and get into a circle and then all turn one way. Each woman then rubs the back of the woman in front of her for a lovely massage. Then, I have people turn the other way and return the favor. So everybody gets two nice back rubs free, and without having gone to the hospital. Women love it. Try that, or try group hugs with your friends or to break up the sitting at some boring meeting.

A social worker once told me that she was running a widows' program in a community of Italian Americans where widows were expected to wear black forever and be very proper. She had planned all sorts of "grief work" for them that she had learned in social work school. However, much to her surprise, the women wanted to tell "dirty jokes." She was smart enough to know that they needed to do this, needed, at least this as a release. There are, as I have said repeatedly, many ways to express ourselves.

Start talking frankly to your women friends, to your husband or lover if you have one, and to your doctor to educate her or him, or to learn. Start being outrageous. Start reading. Be aware of AIDS and venereal diseases. Protect yourself if you are active with more than a faithful lifetime partner. Use good judgment about with whom you are alone and with whom you are intimate.

Don't feel yourself a failure if you can't find a man in later years and want to. It is not that there is anything wrong with you; it is the demographics. If you want a man, go where the men are. You won't find them in activities that appeal only to women. One seventy year old woman met her new husband at a football game. If you can't find a partner, get all the fringe benefits of celibacy. You'll have to pick up only your own socks and wash one pillowcase.

What do you do if you are interested in a man younger than you? Do you slap your wrists and say "he's not for me, I am too old." Nonsense. You are, as a woman, a long liver since women live about eight years longer than men. It is totally appropriate that you partner with a younger man. It is insurance that you will not lose him to death soon. If he reciprocates and you two are compatible, it is silly to count years. One of the women in my poetry workshop, at seventy, has a great erotic relationship with a fifty-nine year old man. Men often slow down before women do. Women are sexually able to function at any age.

Whatever you do, realize you are a grown up. What you do is your business and your choice. Whether it is a younger man, a woman, or self stimulation and pleasuring or other ways of fulfilling yourself, you are in charge, not some "they" out ·there telling you what to do.

*
* *

Sexuality Resources

Growing Older, Getting Better by Jane Porcino, Addison Wesley, Reading, MA, 1983. See the chapter titled "Sexuality and Intimacy as We Age," and the chapter on menopause. Includes a list of resources.

Paula Brown Doress and Diana Laskin Siegel and the Midlife and Older Women's Book Project. *Ourselves Growing Older*, Touchstone Books, Simon and Schuster, 1987. **New edition expected 1993-1994.**

Boston Women's Health Book Collective. *Our Bodies, Ourselves: A Book by and for Women*. New York: Simon and Schuster, 1984. See chapters on sexuality and women growing older.

Brecher, Edward M., and the Editors of Consumers Union. *Love, Sex and Aging*. Boston: Little Brown, 1984.

Butler, Robert and Lewis, Myrna. *Love and Sex After Sixty: A Guide for Men and Women in Their Later Years*. New York: Harper and Row, 1986. This is a revised and enlarged edition of their book published in 1976. It is also available in a large print edition.

"Sexuality in Later Life," an issue of the *Journal of Geriatric Psychiatry* (Vol. XVII, No. 2 1984), has helpful information in it. This journal is available from International Universities Press, Inc., 315 Fifth Avenue, New York, NY 10016. It can also be found in University and hospital libraries.

The Widow's Handbook: A Guide for Living, Charlotte Foehner and Carol Cozart, Fulcrum, Golden, California, has some down to earth advice about widows dating, sexual intimacy, and remarriage in chapter "Taking Care of Yourself, Getting Out and About."

Zilbergeld, Bernie, *Male Sexuality*, Boston, Little Brown, 1978. Highly recommended by the authors of *Ourselves Growing Older*.

Comfort, Alex, *Joy of Sex*, New York, Crown, 1972.

Dodson, Betty, *Liberating Masturbation*, published by Betty Dodson, Box 1933, Murray Hill Station, New York, NY 10156.

Olds, Sally Wendkos, *The Eternal Garden: Seasons of Our Sexuality*, New York, Times Books, 1985.

Ranshohoff, Rita, M. Ph.D., *Venus After Forty*, New Horizon Press, Far Hills, N.J., MacMillan Publishing Company, 1987.

Hammond, Doris B., *My Parents Never Had Sex: Myths and Facts of Sexual Aging*, Golden Age Books, Prometheus Books, Buffalo, NY 1987.

Solnick, Robert, ed., *Sexuality and Aging*, University Park, California, Andrus Gerontology Center, University of Southern California, 1978. Articles about sex and aging including nursing home and health care perspectives.

Starr, Bernard and Marcella Weiner, *The Starr Weiner Report on Sex and Sexuality in the Mature Years*.

Sex Over Forty, Periodical; Order from S/40 PO Box 40428, San Antonio, TX 78229.

Sex and The Female Ostomatic, pamphlet from United Ostomy Association, Inc., 20001 W. Beverly Blvd., Los Angeles, CA 90057.

Sex and Heart Disease, order from your local chapter of the American Heart Association or the national center, 7320 Greenville Ave., Dallas, TX 75231.

Turner, Barbara F. and Catherine Adams, "The Sexuality of Older Women" in *Older Women*, edited by Elizabeth Markson, Lexington, MA, D.C. Heath, Lexington Books, 1983.

Bachrach, Lonnie, *For Each Other*, New York, Anchor Doubleday, 1982. Recommended by authors of *Ourselves Growing Older* as a book for couples to practice sexual intimacy through communication exercises.

Kaplan, Helen Singer, *The New Sex Therapy*, in New York, Brunner Mazel, 1984. Medically oriented with information on medication as related to sexual functioning.

Loulan, JoAnn, *Lesbian Sex*, San Francisco, Spinsters Ink, 1984.

Jacobs, Ruth Harriet, *Button, Button, Who Has the Button?*, poetic drama about older women's lives including their sexuality. Available from the author or KIT Publishing, Inc., 1131-0 Tolland Turnpike, Suite 175, Manchester, CT 06040 $13.95 plus $2 mailing.

Jacobs, Ruth Harriet, *Older Women Surviving and Thriving*, Family Service America, 11700 West Lake Park Drive, Milwaukee, WI 53224. This is a manual for group leaders and includes a session on sexuality and an alphabet of older women's sexuality options.

ORGANIZATIONS

American Association of Sex Educators, Counselors and Therapists. 11 Dupont Circle, NW Route 220, Washington, D.C. 20036. Sex information and Education Council of U.S., 80 Fifth Ave., Suite 801, New York, NY 10011.

FILMS/VIDEOTAPE

Rose by Any Other Names, 15 minute presentation of sexual activity and sanctioning in a nursing home. Good discussion starter. Available from Multi-Focus, Inc., 1525 Franklin St., San Francisco, CA 94109. Phone 800-821-0514.

Sexuality and Aging, one hour videotape from the University of Nebraska Film Library, $55 plus mailing. (Lincoln, Nebraska).

* *
*

An Alphabet of Ways of Expressing Sexuality for Older Women

There are only twenty-six letters in the alphabet; thus only twenty-six styles of sexual expression are given here. Actually, there are many more kinds of sexual expression, and this alphabet is only a sampler of possibilities. You many not find yourself or your particular style here. You might find that you combine aspects of several of the styles presented. Each woman's style is presented very briefly, and more could be said about each of them.

ANNE, who is married, has sexual intercourse with her husband although not as frequently as in earlier years. They enjoy their sexual activity very much. Anne and her husband have a longer period of foreplay than they did formerly because it takes him longer to achieve an

---

The above resource listing is a sampler only. A good library will yield many more publications and resources.

erection. Sometimes they have oral sex, which works well for them. They asked their doctor for information about positions and techniques that are more comfortable for older people. Among these are that Anne stimulates her husband's genitals with her caresses and he stimulates her as well. Anne uses K-Y jelly as a clitoral and vaginal lubricant although her friend, Sara, uses a prescription item her doctor recommended.

BARBARA, who is single, has a male friend who generally spends one night a week at her apartment and shares her bed. She has known him for several years, having met him at the senior center shortly after his wife died. Sometimes they vacation together.

CAROL has been unable to find a male partner although she would like to. She self-pleasures to relieve her sexual tension. Carol has read that about twenty-five percent of older women do so, including some whose husbands are no longer sexually active with them.

DOROTHY has been a lesbian all of her life, and she continues to have a sexual relationship with the woman who has been her lifetime partner.

EVELYN, in younger years, had relationships with men. Now she meets few available men, and she satisfies her sexual needs with other women.

FRIEDA is close to her women friends and shares good and bad times with them. But she does not have sexual relationships with them and would not consider this although she finds it nice to touch and hug her women friends. They all enjoy the human warmth and comforting.

GERTRUDE never did really enjoy her sexual life. Having recently divorced, she is relieved not to be bothered with sex. She gets along very well without it. So does her friend, Glenda, a lifelong celibate who is happy with her situation.

HELEN, a widow, misses romance but has not met anyone her age who is both suitable and single. Anyway, her moral views include the conviction that sex should only be a part of marriage. She does enjoy reading novels and short stories about the sexual experiences of others and likes movies that have sexual themes.

IDA, a widow, misses being touched and gets a health massage once a week. She also takes bubble baths to relax and sometimes dances alone to records.

JUDITH hopes to find a male partner. She puts ads in a singles magazine seeking a nice, respectable man of seventy years of age, who likes quiet evenings at home. In the meantime, she self-pleasures.

KATHERINE attends dances. She talks and dances with men she meets there and enjoys this very much. But she goes home alone. She does not want involvement.

LILLIAN also goes to dances and enjoys dancing with men. Sometimes Lillian goes to a singles club for older adults where she meets men. When she likes a man and knows him well enough to be sure he is trustworthy, Lillian invites him home, and they might have sex.

MARILYN accepts celibacy in her old age. She makes sure that she gets plenty of exercise. She loves nature and enjoys taking long walks. Marilyn keeps busy by volunteering at church and elsewhere.

NORA and her friends enjoy telling "off-color" jokes. They also talk about their past romances, having none now in their lives.

OPHELIA says her relationship with her husband was wonderful and nobody will ever take his place. She has two cats to which she gives lots of attention. Ophelia keeps busy with lots of hobbies.

PRISCILLA plays the piano whenever she gets tense. She likes romantic songs.

QUEENIE remarried recently at seventy-five years of age to an eighty-one-year-old man. "We are like kids," she says.

ROBERTA enjoys swimming at the YWCA, where she likes the intimacy of the locker room. Women are uninhibited there, and it is okay to be nude – wrinkles, bulges, and all. Now single, she revels in the freedom from the many responsibilities that she had in her marriage.

SALLY meets her sensual needs by eating and cooking, as well as gardening and handling beautiful flowers. She also loves fabrics and sewing. Sally enjoys children, so she babysits for the infants and children of her friends and neighbors. She loves to pat babies and children and kiss their soft heads.

THELMA reads magazines and books that are very erotic, even pornographic. She laughs that she now has to hide things from her grown children, instead of the other way around as when they were adolescents at home

UNA, who is in a nursing home, has a very close relationship with a man in the home. They kiss and touch whenever they have a chance and spend as much time together as possible. They would like the comfort of sharing a bed and wish the staff were less opposed to this.

VERA has a much older husband who is an invalid. Sexual acts are not possible for him, but she gives him lots of tender, loving care. Vera bathes her husband gently, brushes his hair, and kisses him. She finds this satisfying.

WILHEMINA worries a lot about the sexual promiscuity of young people today. She spends a lot of time at church praying for them. She tries not to think about sex herself.

XIMENA paints very romantic pictures full of lovers and flowers and daydreams about love.

YVETTE has a husband who says he is not interested in sex anymore. Yvette has made arrangements for the two of them to get counseling at a family service agency. Yvette checked with her family doctor who advised her that her husband has a psychological hangup about aging. Recently, Yvette has read some books on the sexuality of older adults.

ZENA gets a lot of pleasure out of dressing attractively, being well groomed, and receiving compliments on her appearance. She loves using cosmetics and perfume. Zena flirts a bit with men of all ages, "harmlessly," as she says. She hopes some day "Mr. Right" will appear, but, in the meantime, she enjoys life.

CHAPTER TWELVE

Being Politically Outrageous

IT ALWAYS UPSETS ME when I meet older women who say they feel useless because their children are grown or they have stopped doing paid work. There is plenty of work for us to do, politically, and in our communities, to see that people are treated decently and that we have a decent society and world peace. I know it seems like a gargantuan task to work on social problems. But Mother Theresa, when confronted with immense problems in India, said she didn't have to succeed, she just had to start working on the problems. You don't have to solve all problems. Pick one and do what you can about it with your energy, time, and money.

As individuals, we can first work to eliminate from ourselves the sexism, ageism, racism, homophobia, and ethnocentricism bred in us by society. We can then work to change others and to change our social institutions. We can work for human kindness and toward peace. Our society is far from perfect. I love my country, as you do, but on July 4, 1990, I wrote the following poem which was printed the following week in the *Wellesley Townsman*, my town newspaper.

> Oh say can you see by the dawn's early light
> how some physicians seduce their patients
> most hospitals and colleges reject the poor
> some college presidents are pornographic
> major mayors and police chiefs are addicts
> armament manufacturers cheat the government
> and produce defective weapons to stockpile
> with all the other unnecessary expensive ones

while the homeless roam the cities seeking
food, a place to sleep and human compassion
that has been metamorphosized into cynicism
reigning in high places and in the hearts
of voters who reject social service taxes.
Condos and savings and loans burst in the air
while credit cards float down over the land
shouting "buy, have, own, consume, pay later
continue to pollute the world with excesses."
Wife abuse, rape and incest are more American
than apple pie. People often abuse even
their own children or their aged parents.
There are very few functional families.
Half of Americans are in Twelve Step Programs
seeking recovery and the other half dull
anxiety in ways not yet recognized or named.
Oh say can you see by the dawn's early light
how sad and dark is this frightening night.

Take half an hour, and write your own poem or prose list of the problems you see in your community, our whole society, or in the world. There is something you can do about at least one of them. Perhaps you want to pick a problem close to home like the way the older women are discriminated against. Some of the discrimination is just that they are not treated as important or bright just because they are female and old. They do not get credit for the way they can manage despite odds.

Old women are smart.
They pull shades
against the sun or cold
to keep a single flower
alive and comforting for weeks.

Old women are frugal.
They take a friendly word

and make a feast.
A warm touch will last
them all winter.

Old women know
when you ignore them.
When you see only their age
not them
they see through you.

As we saw in chapter six, even doctors who do not take their complaints or needs seriously discriminate against old women. Older women find it hard to get jobs or keep them because of ageism. Now society is cutting back on services which allow many older women to survive—services like home health aides and homemakers which let frail old women stay in their own homes to receive care with dignity.

A few years ago, after hearing case after case of how older women are discriminated against, individually and collectively, in the health care system and in society generally, I went into a fit of depression and wrote a science fiction story. I later read it aloud to shake up the International Association of Gerontology members attending a conference titled "Realistic Expectations for a Long Life." I had been asked to speak probably because I am usually outrageous and funny on the platform, but, by the time I finished the speech, people were pretty upset. That's what I intended. We have to fight ageism now before it gets worse.

To shake you up so you will start fighting ageism, especially against us older women, I am putting that story, *One in Twenty*, in this chapter. Please read it even if you don't like science fiction. A shorter version of the story was published in the excellent older women's magazine, *Broomstick*.

*
* *

My poem above appeared in *Old Hickory Review*, Jackson, TN, 1987 Senior Citizen Edition.

In the nation of A.S.U., in the year 2000, planning began. Dr. Demo Graph was installed in the sacred, secret place of the Miracle Computer which could unleash the nuclear might of A.S.U. The President's advisers were thrilled that the multi-trillion dollar computer contained a subsidiary program to allow Dr. Demo Graph to know the exact second when one in twenty would occur. That way, Miracle's cost could be attributed to the human service budget rather than to the defense budget.

It was Dr. Graph's task, when one in twenty was reached, to start operation C.R.O.N.E. by sending orders throughout A.S.U.

One in twenty referred to the fact that persons over age 85 had become one in twenty of the population. C.R.O.N.E. was an acronym for Can Remove Older Nuisances Efficiently. Older Nuisances were defined as *women* over 85 who dramatically outnumbered old men and who were thought less valuable, even while young, than males.

It was decided that when one in twenty occurred, fast action would ensue. To prepare, a team of historians, psychologists, physicians, gerontologists, sociologists, movement specialists, and removement specialists had been assembled, trained, equipped, and sworn to secrecy. Recruits had been instructed that patriotism required eliminating the expense caused by the daily life and medical needs of older nuisances. Thus, there would be more resources for the fourth generation Star Wars system. Staff was well paid and honored, and their re-socialization was thorough.

Daily, they were shown slides from medical journal advertisements as far back as the 1970's depicting older women as depressed, helpless, fatuous, out of contact, silly, and engaging in meaningless, trivial, passive, noncontributory pursuits. "Are these folks you would want around?" they were asked.

Also shown daily, were movies, comic strips, cartoons, and television commercials of past decades featuring older women as ridiculous. The commercials had been sponsored by such mainstream institutions as telephone companies and chain restaurants. Trainees also studied excerpts from past adult and juvenile literature portraying older women as irrelevant, meddlesome, and stupid at best and, more often, as malevolent.

"We think they stink," was offered as a hypothesis, and this became a scientific theory by smell tests of old women whose incomes were so low or nonexistent that they lived on the streets or in rooms without bathing facilities. A repugnant spray was developed called essence of crone and was sprayed at project meetings. Attractive, happy, older women were never shown or discussed.

Whenever a trainee suggested that his Great Grandmother or neighbor was different, he was assured that this was a rare exception or that the crone in question would inevitably reach senility. Slogans were repeated and flashed subliminally with such messages as "crones may seem alive but at eighty-five they take a dive," and "crones may look alright but they are a fright."

A CRONE of the Day was depicted on a large screen. She was usually a nursing home patient with vacant face and beseeching, reaching arms and a mouth labelled "greedy." Once a women trainee said that crones of the day looked over medicated and isolated. The trainer admitted that was true. However, he stated, crones liked this. "Moreover, tranquilizers and segregated care cost money, and attendant time is better spent on missiles," he said.

He also threatened the trainee or other "crone lovers" with being assigned to bed and body work on crones if they were fond of them. The trainer told the trainee an attendant's salary would prevent a decent standard of living and that she would be a low status outcast doing unimportant work. The trainee never again dissented.

All the data about the many vital, self-sufficient, and helpful older women were lost or reinterpreted by sophisticated, statistical techniques as not valid.

After complete orientation, the specialists went to work using the techniques of their disciplines. The historians were especially helpful because they found useful information in archives. The documents of the holocaust were most valuable, but there were also concepts and methods retrieved from the Spanish Inquisition, the Armenian massacres, the annals of slavery and black genocide, Hiroshima, the relocations of certain hyphenated citizens in World War II, Vietnam, West Philadelphia, the Crusades, and many other events. The persecution and killing of so-called witches on various continents was elucidating.

Each team had its task. The sociologists, psychologists, and communication experts planned for public cooperation through crone posters, the mass media, billboards, electronic devices, and new 21st century techniques for C.O.M.P. (Compliance On Matters Political.)

In view of history, not much opposition was anticipated but precautions were taken. Team players said, "To be base, we will cover the bases." Indeed, humor was generally pervasive. Team members competed with jokes about stupid, useless crones. Anyone who developed a new crone joke was assured a day off and possibly a bonus. Good jokes were used in anti-crone booklets prepared for the public. The historians were lucky because they were able to dig up old mother and mother-in-law jokes and strengthen those. Polish and moron jokes were resurrected too.

English majors, philosophy majors, artists, songwriters, and many others who had been unable to get jobs before project C.R.O.N.E. worked on materials. Anthropologists and gerontologists cooperated with the sociobiologists to prove that ice floes, dying rocks and potions, and neglectful long term care institutions of primitives were natural and desirable societal evolutionary mechanisms. In fact, one anthropologist received a Presidential medal for documenting that the Noah's Arc syndrome, named by sociologist Ruth Jacobs in 1979 as the way widows and older divorcees were treated, was a functional mechanism to protect social intercourse from contamination by pre-crones and crones. That old men preferred young women was seen as further substantiation of a functional thesis of societal purity maintenance.

Because the operation was initially secret, strong bonding and elitism emerged among project C.R.O.N.E. personnel; their crone contempt and hatred was intense. When project C.R.O.N.E. was finally announced, the staff became role models in their communities. Later, when anti-crone propaganda was disseminated widely, crone baiting grew rapidly everywhere in A.S.U., throughout its sphere of influence, and even among its enemies. Anti-crone songs were translated into all languages.

Old women had been shunned in A.S.U. and elsewhere, but now they were actively despised and feared. Crones were blamed for all social problems and for national debts though truly they were powerless, and little was spent on them except for project C.R.O.N.E. It became dangerous to associate with crones. Crone sympathizers were labelled cronies and penalized. Anti-crone T shirts were fashionable. Coloring of grey hair, use of cosmetics, plastic surgery, and lying about age, always important in A.S.U., became intensified. Crones went out only at dark, and many were injured. Windows were broken in what little crone housing was left after the era that began with President Nagaer (1981–1988). Crones were finally legally restricted from public places. This made it hard for crones to organize on their own behalf. Also, historically, in the A.S.U., many older women had internalized negative images, had low self-esteem, and identified with detractors, not peers. They rejected other crones while claiming themselves not to be crones.

Various self pride movements of crones had arisen as early as the 1970s, and there continued to be individuals and groups of courageous and notable activists. An organization called C.A.N. (Crones Against Negation) demonstrated heroically. Some young crony sister-travelers helped. However, enormous funds from certain sources were poured into a counter organization call CAN'T (Come and Nix Them.) The leader of CAN'T was a seventy-five year old woman carefully recruited and prompted, and well rewarded. In earlier years, she had prospered by helping destroy the fourth wave of feminism. She said that C.A.N. really stood for Criminals and Nuts and that C.A.N.S. should be stacked in jails and mental hospitals for society's protection and for their rehabilitation. "They are paranoid fanatics" she said. Her advice was taken.

Meanwhile, Dr. Demo Graph continued to monitor Miracle Computer. Into Miracle went all census material, records of births and deaths, etc. The ratio of 85 year olds rose steadily despite further cutbacks in Social Security, SSI, medical care, and housing and despite the suicides among sensitive, depressed, or "socially responsible" crones. Crones who suicided were celebrated, and their cooperative families honored. However, insufficient crones or families followed this course. "Should we sacrifice children's needs to those of crones?" reached others. "There will be more for the 65 and 75 year olds," persuaded doubters. Of course, nobody leaked the secret. Miracle Computer had been re-programmed to alert when the ratio of over 75 year old crones reached a certain amount, a point not distant. Sons of Dr. Demo Graph and new specialists were at work preparing for this and for, if

necessary, the over 65 year old croning. There had been some suggestion that over 85 and 75 year old males be removed first, but it was
decided this was inappropriate and unthinkable. The relatively few
males were a national treasure, after all.

The society was not without compassion. A museum was set up
to honor crones who gave their lives for defense. It contained wheel-
chairs, granny chairs, crutches, the ads from the medical journals,
Grandmother's Day cards, and the advertisements, books, movies, and
other artifacts mentioned earlier. It did not contain, however, the
many journals and poems that crones had written or the records of all
crones had done for families, community, and economy. As far as possible, these were incinerated along with the crones.

However, one man who had been influenced by a gerontology
course taught by a near-crone, managed to retain his Grandmother's
journal. When orders went out so the over 75 year old crones were
removed, he used his skill as a computer hacker to get her last journal
entry onto computers everywhere. He would be punished, but felt
compelled. His Grandmother's statement, flashed on Miracle Computer and other screens, was:

> First you denied us equality because we were women.
> Then, you hated us because we were *old* women.
> You treated us as invisible and saw only our ages.
> We had much to share but you did not want it.
> You saw your own mortality on our faces.
> Your failures were reflected by our eyes
> Which saw your weakness, deceit and madness.
> You turned from us and your humanity to inhumanity.
> You became infatuated with destructive technology.
>
> We had much to tell about loving ways to live
> And of nurturance for people everywhere
> But you were afraid to see or hear us.
> Now, you will never know what we might have taught.
> We love you even as we are moved and know very well
> What loving means. We are not stupid. We do hurt.

We will weep for you as we are removed.
Who will weep for our lost sunrises?
Who among you, will be the next to follow us?

end of story

*   *
*

Now, my crone story is, of course, a satire, not necessarily prophetic of what may happen. But there are so many cutbacks in social services and such growing reluctance in the society to help others, that many kinds of Americans are already being treated as expendable. Years ago, few people would have predicted that we, as a society, would tolerate the many thousand homeless people we, as a society, are growing callous about.

Operation CRONE is already happening in subtle ways as medical services for the old are rationed. You might want to join with the Older Women's League, the Gray Panthers or other organizations to work in advocacy for older people. Or you may have some other cause to work on. Rather than being outraged, get out of the rage eating you by expressing it in political action such as letter writing to political leaders and government officials, picketing, telephoning, creative protests that occur to you. You will get a high from activism whether it is getting names on a petition or using your contacts and skills in other ways. Because you are a seasoned woman, you are smart. Use older woman power collectively with other women. We have little to lose and a lifetime of anger at injustices and wrongs to work out. Doing it will make us good models for younger people including our descendants.

I would not presume to tell you what cause to choose, besides fighting ageism, my special focus in this book. You will find your place and the way and make a dent, even if you don't change the world. Erik Erikson, a ninety year old psychologist, has written about the integrity of old age that makes us know our lives were and are worth living. The opposite of integrity, he points out, is despair. Rather than despair at the wrongs of the world, we can work on them in whatever limited imperfect ways we can. It is very therapeutic to take even a little action.

It is much healthier than focusing on your own troubles or aches and pains. You should be good to yourself, but being good to yourself also means caring about the world in which you and future generations will live.

CHAPTER THIRTEEN

Having Fun

AFTER that serious chapter on political action and advocacy, you may be feeling pretty grim. But the truth is you can have a lot of fun being a thorn in the flesh of those who do not do right by you or others. You have a sense of humor which can sustain you through tough times. I had the pleasure of knowing the late Saul Alinksky, a social reformer. He told hilarious stories of how he combined fun and social action.

Saul did a lot of work on poverty in Rochester, N.Y. Once, he wanted the wealthier people of the city to take notice of the needs of the poor, not ignore them. So he bought a lot of tickets to the symphony concert. Before he took the large number of poor people to the concert, he fed them a baked bean supper to add their gas sounds to the music. Another time, he drove a bank, which was discriminating, to reconsider its policies by getting sizeable numbers of people to go into the bank, open an account, and then later that day, go back and close it. The lines tied up the bank completely. The bank got the point.

You can have fun even just for the sake of fun. We all need vacations from being serious. Real vacations where we go away are great. So are mini-vacations when we stop taking ourselves and the world seriously. On Halloween, I go to the supermarket and do my shopping wearing the most hilarious costume I can invent. A wonderful gerontologist named June Hall dresses now and then as a clown, and becomes one. A sixty year old educator, Marilyn Bentov, has taken up a late career as a story teller. Sylvia Fee, a landscape architect, has parties where people receive silly prizes for silly sayings. My Friend's Women's group has a meeting every once in a while where we tell funny stories instead of dealing with personal or political issues of weight. I have a collection of funny masks I sometimes put on when I am giving talks. People get others to laugh by wearing funny buttons. You can think of lots of things, too. I went to a week of intense workshops at the 1990 International Women's Writing Guild. We spent a lot of time writing together and reading aloud what we wrote. People wrote profound things, and I certainly tried to, also. However, I really don't remember those profound things. What I remember is the things that made me laugh or at least smile. People tell me that what they remember is not the poems where I tried to be profound but the silly or seemingly trivial ones like the one I wrote about my nose.

> This nose can smell lavender, lilacs, lies and a louse.
> This nose can point to garage sales with prizes
> Great enough to make your nose twitch with envy.
> This nose can smell out snobs, secrets and storms.
> This nose can sense decay beneath erotic perfumes
> And knows when other noses turn up in disdain
> Above false smiling mouths and insincere tongues.
>
> This nose has memories of sea mists and trysts
> Nine months before the smell of baby flesh and diapers.
> This nose is a diary of 66 years and leads onward
> Sniffing out outrageous scenes and wonderful people
> With sweet sweat, heart flowers and honest noses.

Spending time with children is a way to keep your sense of humor intact. Ruth Hoge, the ninety-five year old in my Friends meeting, gives wonderful serious messages to the adults in the meeting. But she says that what is very important to her about the meeting is being active in the children's classes. Children are often spontaneously and wonderfully silly. This is something we can all emulate. What adult has not felt better after laughing with a child or making a baby laugh? Older women who do not have little descendants or ones who live nearby need to find ways to make contacts with children through neighboring, volunteering, baby sitting.

We also need to find ways to amuse each other. Two women in their seventies have a contest I love. They compete each Christmas to see who can give each other the tackiest Christmas present wrapped in the most outrageous way. It is the highlight of the holiday. I buy crazy, useless things at garage sales to amuse my friends. I once wrote a poem about frogs. I like frogs. My family and friends turn up hilarious frogs for me, the weirder the better. My son got into the act and produced a huge frog statue.

Develop your sense of playfulness. By the time we are 65, most of us have five chronic conditions. Nobody really wants to hear about them, especially in detail. You will be much more popular if you have amusing stories to tell about your own foibles. You can even poke fun at others if it is done kindly. People like the attention of being picked on if the picking on is good humored and funny and not in a sensitive area.

For a long time, I would only permit myself to read magazines when I was on a plane. I found myself eagerly grabbing several the minute I got on the plane, even before I found my seat. If I were on a long trip and finished these, I would go get more if they were in the bin. If the magazines were gone, I would go up and down the aisles seeing who had finished and would trade their magazines for mine. At home, I would only permit myself to read serious books and journals. Finally, I realized that I liked some light reading to counteract the heavy and that I had a right to be entertained and amused. So I started to read magazines when at the public library getting my serious books. Eventually, I graduated to subscribing to a few of my favorite fun magazines.

You may have some area too in which you are not indulging yourself because of a feeling you are not entitled to pleasure or fun. Think about it. If not now, when? My friend Laura Ferguson said a very wise thing to me. At nearly 80, she realized she had always lived for the future and that it was time to start living for today. This especially resonated with me. Several years ago I lost a friend from high school who was, at sixty-five, working too hard at a full time job, saving up money so that, eventually, she could retire and have lots of travel money. It would have been better if she had done some easing up and enjoyed travel and life along the way. Perhaps, then, she would not have had a heart attack. Her sizeable estate went to a distant cousin as my friend had no descendants.

Some women think it outrageous to spend money on themselves. They will give their descendants money or generous gifts and keep the thermostats in their houses so low that they risk hypothermia, becoming ill or even dying from the cold. They will give up vacations or cancel plans so that they can be available in case adult children need them for babysitting, advice, or whatever. I understand that completely. I, too, had the pink blanket thrown over me at birth and was taught that women nurture everyone else. My daughter jokingly reminded me the other day that I tell her where I will be every two minutes when I travel. She is thirty-five, capable, and has lots of friends. Old habits die hard.

Many of us older women, brought up in another era, feel we can't have friends in to visit unless our houses are spotless, and we can provide a feast. This is ridiculous and keeps us isolated. We need to invite our friends to come potluck style and to enjoy our dust balls. We might develop a competition along the lines of my house is messier than yours and give prizes to the most relaxed housekeepers among us.

I loved the fact that one friend, a struggling novelist, suggested we could have a gathering at her house. Instead of everyone having to bring potluck stuff, one of us could pick up take-out Chinese food on the way, and we could split the cost. It was a pleasure not to have to worry about what to cook or to worry about cooking it. The evening was that much more enjoyable because we knew that our hostess would have no mess to clean up and that her slim pocketbook was out only the cost of tea bags and paper plates. We wouldn't let her pitch in for the inexpensive food.

My dear friend Edith Stein, retired now from her job directing Foster Grandparents in Boston, knows how to give great parties. For her sixty-fifth, she invited all her friends and said they were to bring no presents, only food or wine to be shared. Edith and her husband, incidentally, have evolved a wonderful lifestyle. Half the year, during the good weather in Boston, they live in their condo and enjoy their friends and relatives and cultural events here. The other half of the year, they rent their condo and use the proceeds to live cheaply in rural France.

My friend, Eleanor, and my daughter gave me a potluck surprise party for my sixty-fifth birthday. They instructed my friends to bring food or wine and to write poems as presents. My friends are not poets. Yet some of them had great fun writing their first poems for this event. I put all the poems in a sixty-five birthday box. In low moments, I take them out and read them. I treasure them much more than I would have treasured gifts that my friends spent their limited money buying. All the poems are wonderful, but I want to share two because they speak to some of the lessons we aging women have to learn. The first was written by Joan Valdina, past seventy, and it was the first poem she ever wrote.

> Gird your loins, this isn't peachy
> it's a sermon and a poem teachy and preachy
> Hope you have so much more
> than just a happy birthday in store.
> Hope you will venture far and near
> and have a rousing birthday year
> one in which you'll finally learn
> that it's better to tarry than to burn
> tarry and sit back on the shelf
> and really get to meet yourself.
> a year in which you'll bravely dare
> to see yourself as someone rare
> and see that now you must dare
> to *enjoy yourself* as a person rare.

I think all older women can learn something from wise crone Joan's poem about valuing and indulging ourselves. The second poem I will share was written by my daughter, Edith Jane Jacobs.

> No Mahjong, no knitting, no retirement in sight
> So what is nigh sixty-five, this November night?
> It's a speeding ticket and pool crashing
> quilt stalking and ageism bashing.
> It's writing and speaking and megamentoring,
> driving cross country, turquoise and beadwork foraging.
> It's creative and smart and learning to receive
> and knowing what to take and what to leave

at garage sales and invitation wise.
It's hard earned and well deserved prestige and long
      standing ties.
This is sixty-five. I'm glad and proud to say:
I love you, Mom, Happy Birthday.

Those of you who are mothers will know how much this poem
meant to me although in it Edith is gently reminding me, like Joan,
to set limits on the world and be good to Ruth. In sharing her poem
and Joan's, I share, I hope, some advice that will be useful to you.

I would also like to share a story I was told that will show you, I
hope, that it is never too late to put your own needs first. A Quaker
woman who has passed her one hundredth birthday still lives alone
and continues to be a source of wisdom and support for those who
drop in on her when they need cheering up. One day, someone went
to call, and this woman came to the door and said, "Sorry, I can't see
you today. Goodbye." The caller, upset, went back to a friend saying,
"She must be getting senile; she was always glad to see me before." The
friend went to call on the old woman a few days later and asked why
the centenarian had refused entry. The old woman replied, "For over
one hundred years I always put other people first and thought I had
to meet everybody's needs, be a good woman. Now, at 104, I have
decided that if I feel like being alone or am busy, I have a right to that."

I hope you will not wait until one hundred and four to put yourself
first, at least sometimes, and to lighten up, have some fun and pleasure
out of life.

CHAPTER FOURTEEN

Prime Time Women's Friendship

P rime time women's friendships
R each deeply and fragrantly
I nto our hearts
M eeting our needs
E nriching our lives.

T ime to find new friends
I n these prime years
M eans support, love
E nergy, growth and hope.

W hy limit your friendships
O r restrict yourself to sameness?
M ake friends of all ages
E specially women older than you
N ecessary models and teachers
S howing you the way.

F ollow your interests,
R reach out to groups,
I nvest in good causes.
E ach place you go,
N ew friends may emerge.
D iscover the joy
S eeking understanding,
H elping and being helped,
I n these later years
P rime and precious.

IN THE ACROSTIC which begins this chapter, I give you a hard sell on the value of friendships with other women. Not only do such friendships sustain us, they also mean that we get along better with our descendants because we are not dependent upon them for companionship. You may already have more friends than you can keep up with and so be tempted to skip this chapter. Before you do, though, I want to ask you to assess whether you have enough friends to fill the various categories below.

Some years ago, the staff of the excellent Human Relations Service in Wellesley, MA, got together to brainstorm on what functions human relationships fill. They came up with a list which one staff member said I could utilize in my work.

Rather than calling them friends, the Human Relations professionals used the term Support System People. Since friends, as well as family, are our support system, you should consider these functions and ask yourself if your friends serve these functions. A given friend does not have to serve them all, but you should have friends to cover all the functions.

The first function is *inclusion*: people who like you, will affirm you. The second is *connectedness*: people who are like you, share your values. The third function is *affirming your competence*: people who know enough about what you do to evaluate your competence. (This third function is especially important when we age; ageist people undermine our self esteem by considering us less competent, and even invisible, because of age.) The fourth function is *crisis overload help*: people who will move in at bad times. People you can ask for help. (Foul Weather Friends.) The fifth function is *intimacy*: close, personal friends; people with whom you can share your fears, joys, defeats, and successes. The sixth function is *stimulation/challenge*: people who challenge and stimulate you.

Some women think the only kind of friends that truly can be called friends are the category five group, intimate friends. You also need the other kinds. Besides, friends, unfortunately, die, move away, get busy, and other things happen. It is dangerous to have only a best friend and no other friends. What would you do if you lost that friend? Or this particular only friend might be busy when you need friendship. One woman who was divorced was very happy when she met a splendid woman who was also divorced. They became close friends, went on vacations together, and fulfilled many of the functions for each other listed above. The trouble was that one re-married and moved away, and the other now had no other friends to fall back upon. She could have retreated and become a loner which would have been sad. Or she could have worked hard to make another best friend which might set her up for another loss. Fortunately, she took the wiser course of working at making a number of friends so that her needs were spread over a larger network.

If you need friends, you might ask how she did this. Well, throughout this book I have suggested activities in which you might get involved, and meet some compatible people. Here are some other suggestions.* Although a few of these suggestions repeat what I have said earlier in this book, I put them in the list so you could have them all together.

1   Go more than half way to make friends. Other women are lonely and shy too, even though they don't seem to be on the surface.

2   Read your local paper and bulletin boards carefully, and go to meetings, events, gatherings, that interest you. It will be there that you find women with your interests. Don't think you can make friends sitting at home.

3   If there is a movie or some event you want to attend, call up a woman you'd like to know better and invite her. She may be grateful,

---

* Some of these appeared in my article "Older Women's Friendships" in *Women, Aging, and Ageism*, Vol. 2 , No. 2, 1990, of the *Journal of Women and Aging* and in the book *Women, Aging, and Ageism*, edited by Evelyn R. Rosenthal, Harrington Park Press, Binghamton, NY, 1990.

but if she can't attend, don't be rebuffed. She may have another plan. Try again. People are grateful if you plan outings and reach out.

4   If you move to a new neighborhood, volunteer to canvass for the United Fund or some other cause. It is a good way to meet your neighbors. Also, ask your reference librarian for a list of local organizations.

5   If you attend a church or temple, go up to women you'd like to meet during the coffee hour. Extend yourself. Serve on committees. Attend social events sponsored by your religious denominations.

6   Take a course. Many are free for over 60. Use whatever women's organizations and networks exist in your geographic area.

7   Organize a potluck supper for women you have met. Maybe they'll become frequent events.

8   Don't limit yourself to women your age. You can mentor younger women. You can learn from older women in preparation for your own aging.

9   Do volunteer work or serve on committees. Get involved in causes. You'll meet friends that way.

10   If you have been hurt by a friend, realize that you may have misunderstood or misperceived, or your friend may have been hurt by you, though it was unintentional. Talk things out with that friend.

11   Join your local chapter of the Older Women's League or start a chapter. The national address: 666 Eleventh Street, N.W., Suite 840, Washington, D.C. 20005.

12   If you are a widow, call the Council on Aging or the Senior Center in your town to find out where there is a widow's program you can attend. You will get help and make new friends.

13   Join an Older Women Surviving and Thriving Workshop. If there isn't one in your area, get the manual by that title at $17.95 plus $2.50 mailing from Families International, 11700 West Lake Park Drive, Milwaukee, WI, or from the author, Ruth Harriet Jacobs, 75 High Ledge Avenue, Wellesley, MA 02181. You'll get help with your prob-

lems and meet new friends. The manual will tell you how to find other women for the group and how to do 12 sessions.

14 Start a support group for older women of some kind other than those mentioned in #13 above. Arrange meeting space at a church, temple, community center, etc.

15 Join or start a Great Books group at your library.

16 See what is going on at the nearest senior center. Don't reject your aging or be snobbish about your age. Older women are great.

17 Develop a variety of friends for different activities. It is dangerous to limit yourself to one best friend because of mobility, mortality, and other reasons that could bring loss.

18 Consider shared living arrangements. Look into them with other women.

19 Realize that lack of privacy is less dangerous than isolation.

20 Realize that you will get along better with your adult children if you have a busy happy life with friends than if you are dependent upon your children for companionship. Your adult children will like you better if you are not demanding. You will give your daughter a gift of not fearing her own older womanhood if you are occupied with friends and activities.

21 Don't wait for an absolutely perfect friend. Nobody is perfect. Not even you.

22 Realize that if you are widowed or divorced, your still married friends may stop including you in coupled events. You have two options. You can ask them to please include you even if you are a single. Insist on paying your own way, not having their husbands pay for you. Or, you can realize that the Noah's Ark syndrome has taken hold and that marrieds often don't include singles. You then must make some new single friends.

23 Realize that if your still married friends have no time to meet you alone; woman to woman, that this quite commonly happens to

widows and divorcees. They may be threatened by your losses or they may genuinely be busy with their husbands, especially if the husbands are retired. Many women report this phenomena so it is not that your friends are particularly callous or that there is anything wrong with you. I have still-married friends that I see now and then, alone or with their husbands, but I depend for companionship and support primarily on other older single women.

24   If you are married, realize that you should include your widowed or divorced friends in parties, not assume they would feel strange. They have the choice of refusing, but, if you don't invite them, you give them no choice and sometimes no social outlet.

25   If you are afraid of approaching people and making friends, consider some brief individual or group therapy to figure out why and to work on this issue.

26   Don't think friends have to be a mirror image of yourself. You can enjoy people very different from you. You are not marrying people when you start friendships. If you find they are not as you thought, you can always withdraw gently.

27   Don't eschew people because you think you will have to do things for them. You may. All but the most casual friendships require some reciprocity. But reciprocity can feel good.

28   Realize that if friends live at a distance, or one of you is housebound, that you can have lovely visits over the telephone or by letter. One of my dearest friends moved some years ago, and I have only seen her twice. But we feel close and write often. Another friend is now on the opposite coast in a California retirement community, but I feel this friendship is so important that I manage to get to California every few years. Since she is eighty-seven, I have made this a priority. But I also have recruited new friends within short distances from my home because face to face contact is important.

29   Don't be afraid of getting involved with your neighbors as some people are. They can become friends. The people across the street from me are younger and follow a different lifestyle, but it was good to make friends and look across at their lights and know that I would do almost

anything for them and they for me. I enjoy their children, and I think the children think of me as dear.

30   Try to get some male friends in your life. These may not be romantic relationships. I consider the husbands of two married friends to be also good friends of mine. It is good to be able to consult them on matters of their expertise, somewhat different from women friends. To have the male point of view helps. I have also made friends of men at work.

31   Let people know your hobbies and avocations. This may provide a basis for friendship, casual if not intimate. If you are a movie buff, there is nothing wrong with having a friend with whom you just go to and discuss movies. I once had a friend that I just went to garage sales with, but we had great fun together. She has moved away, but I remember our fun Saturdays when I look at the "treasures." We still mail each other garage sale gifts. A woman who liked to play Scrabble put up a notice in the community center, and found some new Scrabble playing friends that way.

No doubt you could add ways to make and cultivate friends to this list. Let us return to some of the reasons for working at it. Women in our society seem to have greater capacity for same sex friends for many reasons which have been explored by other writers such as Lillian Rubin in her book *Just Friends* (Harper and Row). Research shows that men *do* things with their friends, bowling, drinking, going to events, etc., while women share feelings and are more self revealing. Even happily married women, as pointed out earlier, often seem to need women friends. Indeed, many women who are spouses of retirees have a special problem. One asked if she could stay after a workshop to talk with me privately. This was her story.

"Now that he is not working, my husband likes me home with him all the time unless we go out together. If I want to visit a woman friend or have some women friends over, he wants to come along or be with us. There are things we, as women, would like to talk about that we are not comfortable talking about in front of him, but he doesn't seem to understand, and I wouldn't dream of hurting his feelings; he is very dear to me."

I suggested she steer her husband toward some hobbies, volunteer work, a part time job, and to situations where he might meet other retired men. He really did not have friends except at his former work or in coupled situations with her. Also I pointed out to her that her self-sacrifice for her husband would eventually turn to resentment and show up someplace in their relationship; she was really doing him no favor by giving up time with women friends. She smiled and agreed. "He also might pre-decease you, and you would need your women friends," I added. Women late in life are much more apt to be alone which is why we need more friends than males for whom the wife is often the lifelong best friend, confidant, and social secretary. Unfortunately, most women will end up widowed though the perk is that they live longer. So they have more need for friends than the men who have wives. Friends confirm our identity, importance, connectedness, usefulness, allow us to ventilate, to feel needed and safe, and fill our hours pleasantly and meaningfully.

Friendship After Fifty

Having friends after fifty
can be real nifty
since hotel rates are shifty
being similar for one or two
and you also can get blue
if waiters say "just one"
seat you in the blinding sun,
give you a stale single bun
and make you want to run.

Taking a friend at six O
is a good way to go
to a course on psych or Poe
or learn how easily to hoe
the older woman's row
in a class where you unload
righteous anger at a toad
who demeaned and mocked you
and other older women too.

At seventy or seventy plus
friends make a welcome fuss
if you are well or sadly ill.
They sweeten almost any pill.
Friends will quickly share
a joy, a loss. They care.
Your friends swap jokes,
tales of old folks,
admire your clothes and kids
and unscrew tough jar lids.

At eighty women friends
visit while your hip mends,
ask you for advice
or what is really nice
or how to get rid of mice
and how much of a spice,
and graciously repeat twice.
If you can no longer drive,
they will see you thrive
by taking you out until five.

At ninety or even more
friends come to your door
to learn about old days
and earlier women's ways.
They know it really pays
to understand how each phase
of a woman's life has niches
that only the great riches
of women's friendships fill,
in youth and when over the hill.

My verse on friendship was previously published in *Women, Aging and Ageism*, op. cit.

CHAPTER FIFTEEN

Handling Outrageous Incidents

HOW CAN YOU outrageously handle incidents that fill you with rage? These are not the major traumas of life, but they are insults to you because you are an older woman, and because you are sometimes alone.

What feels insulting is inappropriate language as when a restaurant hostess or waiter says "just one." Instead of meekly nodding, you might, for the shock value and to educate that person say, "isn't one enough." However, there is outright discrimination when you or your party of older women are seated at undesirable tables. You can head that off by specifying at the outset where you want to sit or by saying the table to which you are led is unsatisfactory. You can imply leaving, and you do have the option of eating elsewhere. There is a myth that old people, especially old women, do not tip well. If you get good service, dispel the myth, but if you are badly treated, speak up and say so.

What do you do in a store if everyone else is waited upon first on the assumption that you, being an old woman, have all the time in the world and that your time is less valuable? You can curdle inwardly and be meek or you can speak up and say, "it is my turn."

If cab drivers pass you by for a man who they think will tip better, you can take their license plate numbers, call the cab company, and complain about age discrimination, saying you will get all your friends and relatives to stop using their cabs unless they treat older women fairly.

Should employers discriminate against you on the basis of age, you

163

can remind them there is federal legislation against age discrimination and threaten or use legal resources. Should automobile dealers or car repair shops attempt to exploit you because they think you are stupid, being an older woman, you can study up, show you are knowledge-able, and refuse to be exploited. You can also use your state Con-sumer Protection Agency to file complaints and get redress if you are exploited.

If your retired husband or other relatives expect you to do all domes-tic chores because you are female, you can refuse, and leave the chores undone so that they will get the point that housework is everyone's job. One retired husband who had been an engineer somehow could not learn how to run simple household appliances like the washer and dryer until his wife just quit. When he needed clean underwear and socks, he learned fast. In order to teach people to do their shares of domestic chores, you may have to change. First, you may have to lower standards. If you think only the way you do it is correct, you will have to do it and rage for the rest of your life. Secondly, you will have to resist impatiently doing it yourself to get it done. But don't turn into a brooder because the partner may not be a mind reader. Say explicitly what the chores are. Make a plan with the people you live with, who will do what. Sometimes it is good to put it in writing.

Some men think wives will resent it if they move into the domestic sphere when they retire, and the truth is, some women do. You will have to decide if you want to share this domain and allow him to participate. If you do, follow some of the suggestions above. If you jealously want to guard your sphere, that is your privilege, but you may feel burdened, and he may feel shut out.

How do you handle it when you tell people your age and they say "you don't look that old." You don't take it as a compliment, remem-bering my poem in chapter one. You tell them there is nothing wrong with being that age, and people of your age are terrific. The question of honesty about age is often raised in my workshops. One woman reported that she moved to a new town and met two women she thought would become friends. The three of them went to lunch together, walking briskly into the restaurant. During the course of lunch, the woman mentioned that she had recently celebrated her seventy-fifth birthday. She saw the other two women, who were probably still in their sixties, stiffen. On the way out, they each took her elbow, treating her as frail which she is definitely not. This woman is a very athletic person, exercises daily and takes vigorous, long walks. She also felt that now they would not become friends. They would think she was too old because of the age discrimination that exists even in those who are old themselves. The woman, who needed new friends, told my workshop she should not have revealed her age.

I can empathize with her feelings, but I don't agree. I think we must have age pride, speak our ages proudly, and, if we sense discrimination, help others deal with it. When her two lunchmates stiffened, I think the woman should have initiated a discussion about age being no barrier, letting them know the difference between functional age, what you can do, and chronological age. She should have told them that women in their eighties and nineties these days continue active lives and that seeing people in their seventies as frail was inappropriate. She might have done these two women a favor because they were probably afraid of aging and were projecting their fears about themselves onto her. Here is my poem you might like to give to young women who ignore or patronize you or treat you inappropriately because of their ageism and fear.

To Young Women

Listen to the old women
you may not want to hear
precisely because you fear
getting old some day
having very little say
being thought in the way
becoming ageism's prey
once they stop your pay.

Listen to Barbara's tale
which made her sad and pale.
On retirement from teaching,
she moved and was reaching
out to make new friends

discounting ageist trends
considering herself an equal
but found always the sequel
was that, *they* seeing her age,
ignored her, creating rage.

Retirement can be bad enough
It is really quite tough
to suffer loss of money
and aging aches aren't funny
but being thought inferior
just because years are superior
creates depression in interior
and pain in your posterior.

When young women tune you out,
you want to shake them and shout
"I am wise because of these years
please give me your patient ears
and you will really hear
how to manage and be clear
about your choices in life.
Ignoring me is a double knife
that cuts knowledge from you
just as it wounds me too."

Because I have so much to give
I could really help you live
so that instead of fearing age
you'd consider it another stage.
Listen please to me on this.
It is so sad and cruel to miss
what old women have to say.
Remember, you'll be old one day.

What do you do when radio, television, newspapers or magazines
have programs, articles, ads or commercials that denigrate old women
or make them look silly? Answer: You write and complain, and get all

your friends to write also. If they are local, you also telephone, and sometimes you picket.

How do you handle it when clubs or other organizations make you feel unwelcome because you are no longer young? Clearly, you continue to attend, if you want to, and raise the issue. Also, you start other organizations that are not ageist. And you look around and join ones that advocate for older people.

What do you do if you want to attend a university program, not as a senior citizen, but as a degree candidate and find you are not admitted because of your age? You refuse to let your self confidence be eroded. You protest this blatant ageism and discrimination. One woman who had been turned down in her fifties by a school of social work demanded and got an appointment with the dean. She demonstrated to him how capable and determined she was. He overruled the admissions' committee. It is not always so easy. Another one, rejected from a doctoral program in her fifties demanded and got an appointment with the dean. He treated her paternally, explaining that the program would be stressful "at her age" and that she really would be better off with lower aspirations. Then he said, "Do you understand now?" She answered, "Yes, I understand, and I will see you in court as I have tape recorded this conversation on the tape recorder in my pocketbook." The next day he called to say he had decided to admit her. She finished the program with distinction and is now the dean of social work at a major university.

What do you do if they call you shrill because you demand your rights? You don't get anxious about being unladylike. You realize that a *man* who fought for his rights would be considered appropriate and that ideas of what is ladylike have been used to control women for centuries. You translate shrill to assertive and smile smugly that you have learned how to be assertive in your later years despite your socialization to be a "good girl" and cave in, fearful of censure.

What is your response when well meaning descendants, other relatives, and friends tell you that there is no point in bucking the system? You point out to them that someone has to buck the system. It is your duty to future generations to exercise the elder function of conscience and gadfly. You give them information to get them to join your outrageousness.

What do you do when friends your age will not go swimming because they say, "I don't look good in a bathing suit?" You give them a course on ageism that turns to self-hatred and self deprivation. You point out that older bodies have served their owners well and are to be worn with pride. You also remind them gently that they are perhaps a bit egocentric thinking everybody is watching them. You also show them how much fun you have swimming, flab, wrinkles, and all.

Similarly, if anyone says "I'm too old for that," you educate them on "never too old." They way I educate people is by showing them my button collection which brings laughs of insight. Here are the buttons I own and proudly wear. The first two were mentioned earlier in this book RASP (Remarkable Aging Smart Person) and Youth Is a Gift of Nature: Aging is a Work of Art. The others are: Getting Better with Age, Older Women's League; The Best Age is the Age You Are; I *am* Acting My Age; Age Isn't Important Unless You're Cheese; How Dare You Presume I'd Rather Be Young; Better Over the Hill than Under It; I'm in the prime of my life; Be patterns, be examples; Superstition #36, Life Begins at 40; I've stopped lying about my age; I'm not over the hill, I'm on a roll; Get Growing. I also wear the button that says LIFE, a Massachusetts organization of nursing home patients whose name is Life Is For Everyone. LIFE brings together nursing home residents to enrich their lives and fight for their good care and rights. In addition, I wear the button of the Gray Panthers, Old and Young United, and the Massachusetts Association of Older Americans. I also wrote a big MOM on a button and turn it upside down to say WOW which stands for the Wonderful Older Women we are now.

These buttons are fun to wear, inform people you meet, and are good conversation starters. It has taken me awhile to make my collection. I would be grateful for any buttons you want to send me. You can find these buttons in various places or even have them made. You can convert advertising or political buttons by gluing paper or plastic tape over them. You might consider selling anti-ageist buttons to support your causes and educate people. It is fun.

Putting anti-ageist and pro-age posters or poems on bulletin boards is also useful. The Older Women's League has a great Older Women's Bill of Rights poster. Use your creativity to make your own posters or poems, showing that being old is not a disgrace and that the word old is fine. Old is not a pejorative. The best thing about working to eradicate ageism in others is that you will work on the latent ageism within you, within all of us. Advocacy will help you develop age pride and self pride.

CHAPTER SIXTEEN

Bereavement: Hurting and Healing

IT CANNOT BE DENIED that there are negative aspects of aging, although in Chapter 18 I will be pointing out some of the positive aspects of aging. The worst thing about aging is the losses we sustain as loved ones die. In this chapter, we will look at ways of handling bereavement. Bereavement is an issue more acute for women than for men; women more often lose a spouse. Because so many women are the survivors and need help on how to survive well, I am giving you a bibliography at the end of this chapter so that you may read more if it is your need.

Being in the Greater Boston area, I have been fortunate enough through the years to know Phyllis Silverman, Ph.D., a pioneer in work on widows. Some of what I say in this chapter is drawn from her writing and speaking, especially from a workshop in January 1991, sponsored by the Brookline, Massachusetts Council on Aging and the Brookline Adult and Community Education Program. Other things I say in this chapter are derived from my own research and work with women, and from my reading and attending many other programs on bereavement. I have not been widowed, and no one who has not had the experience can totally understand. However, I have lost a child so I have some knowledge of grief.

Young women lose husbands, especially in war time, and this is very difficult. These are off-time deaths, and young deaths are terrible. However, it is also difficult for older widows, as you know and as we saw in the cases of the widows in chapter six who sought help from their physicians. Often, they are expected to recover quickly from a devastating loss. In losing husbands, they have lost not only a companion, sexual partner, and housemate, but also someone around whom they have structured their lives. Besides the loss of a loved one, women often lose the person who handled finances, did household repairs or knew how to get them done, and did other tasks that in earlier more gender-specific times were assigned to males. At the time when she is reeling from her loss, the older woman must suddenly cope with income tax, estate handling, etc.

The problem of loneliness is compounded for many widows. They may have devoted themselves to a retired husband or to a husband who was ill for many years and needed constant care. One widow reported that, for eight years, her husband had been ill, and she had devoted every waking moment to him. She said "I had formerly, for many years, been an active woman in many organizations and had many women friends whom I saw when my husband was at work. But when he became ill, I gave up all my friends and activities to care for him, for he needed every bit of care I gave. Now I feel like an empty shell. I have no motivation to do anything, and I really no longer have friends to do things with."

The recommendation to her was that she join the widows' support group that was being formed in her town. She would be able to make new friends in this group. Many cities and towns do have these groups which allow people to grieve together and then go on, hopefully together.

There are also widow-to-widow programs which are organized not around group meetings, but through one widow who has moved along working on a one to one basis with a new or unresolved widow, and bringing to her the resources she needs. A marvelous woman, widowed herself, Betty Davis, heads up the widowed services program of the American Association of Retired Persons. She may be contacted at 601 E Street, N.W., Washington, D.C. 20049 about the program nearest you or about how to organize one. A trainer will be sent to help a local community start such a program.

One thing the widow has to learn from these groups or elsewhere is that her symptoms are normal. Too many times our social network expects us to recover before we can. Our family and friends do not want to see our tears, listen to us, or hear about our deceased. We need to talk to people who will understand and who know that grieving takes a long time, and that we may always feel loss. Even if we re-marry, we cannot wipe out the attachment to someone who was a vital part of our life in so many ways.

We have to express our grief. It is not abnormal to be angry and non-functional and to have ways of behaving including strange symptoms that are not part of our normal way of behaving or feeling. As Phyllis Silverman says, "You feel something is wrong with you because you're not doing something right just as your world is crumbling. . . . You should be entitled to scream if you want to without someone jabbing you with a needle."

But Silverman also points out that, though bereavement never ends, it does eventually get manageable. A new phase of life, or what she calls accommodation, begins where the widow goes on to re-arrange her life. She says, "Widows carry the past with them, but ultimately grief doesn't run them. After the impact, when there is numbness and unreality, there is a terrible pain period when people can't stop crying, can't get mobilized, are depressed, but eventually the accommodation brings a time for growing."

Silverman points out that, eventually, many women discover within themselves a new voice that is exciting because it is the voice of their own competency. I have seen this happen many times. Denying first, then devastated, discouraged and depressed widows, sometimes with help, move to using strength and skills. It helps a good deal if they are imbedded in units of belongingness as discussed in chapter nine and have good friends. If they do not have this, they may put undue burdens on their children. One widow estranged her daughter by asking her to build an apartment onto her house for her and to take her on all the daughter's family vacations. She said, "You have to do this now that I am alone." This was a financially and physically able widow who could and should use other ways of re-integrating with people. Fortunately, this widow, angry at her daughter for not complying, was directed to a social worker who helped her see she had to take responsibility for her life and make new relationships.

People who belong to a supportive religious community are often helped by rituals around the death and get continued support from fellow congregants and clergy. Sadly though, the period of concern may be too brief and the help insufficient. In one of his early congregations, Dr. Philip King, director of pastoral counselling at the Massachusetts General Hospital, started a group whose members provided sustained services to older persons in need. He points out, "In times of loss and grief, we need ritual and commitment." Unfortunately, not all congregations have this kind of continued help to the bereaved.

Anniversaries of the death of a spouse can be a re-awakening of the pain. Friends and family should rally to help the widow at that time while the widow herself should realize that strange behavior at that time of the year is normal. I now understand, though I did not the first few years, why I get depressed in the beautiful month of June in New England when one should feel good to see the glories of nature. June was the month my child died. Even, after many years, though I consciously forget the date, June reminds me. So, too, the widow may be reminded by the anniversary of the death, the anniversary of the wedding, the spouse's birthday, etc. It is natural to feel sadness when a new grandchild is born that the dead spouse will not be able to grandparent.

How you move from disabling grief to enabling your life to continue is the question many widows ask. The readings at the end of this chapter may help, but let me give you some advice here that has come from widows and other bereaved I have seen hurt and heal enough to go on and even enjoy life.

1 Express, don't repress, your grief. If you can talk to friends, good counsellors, relatives, the clergy, that can be helpful. Don't isolate yourself. But when you need to cry and be alone, do so.

2 Take Phyllis Silverman's good advice, "Don't look at bereavement as an illness, but rather as part of the life cycle and think, "What can I do about it?"

3 Educate yourself about the functions your spouse performed such as handling finances. Take an AARP or other course on women's financial management.

4 Seek out support groups, and work at making new friends if your

old friends are unavailable, unsympathetic, or so coupled they leave you out. (See chapter 14.)

5   If you are of suitable age and it is possible, get a paid job. (See chapter 17.) Or do volunteer work. Structure in your life is helpful and so is the feeling of being needed. Shortly after I lost my child, I started to do volunteer work with disabled veterans at the veterans' hospital. I found persons worse off than I, and it helped me to help them.

6   Don't expect too much too soon. Five or more years is not too long to recover partially from the terrible loss.

7   Celebrate the positive aspects of having had a long marriage, and remember the good times you had. One widow, Verna Skinner of Connecticut, a volunteer trainer in the AARP Widowed Persons Service, made a scrapbook, a photo album of her life with her husband which comforted her. She is now making one of her own life so her descendants will have it. Talk about the person who is gone. Don't pretend, or let others pretend, he never existed.

8   Since you have lost your wife role and status, seek out new roles and statuses, many of which have been explored in this book. Find people and causes where you can make a difference and where people will care that you are around.

9   If you have any guilt about the deceased, work that through in therapy or through religion.

10   Just keeping busy helps many widows after the first period of intense mourning. One widow who is not well still forces herself to go every day to the hot lunch program at her senior center and finds being with people and the nourishing food helps. Another gets away from her aloneness and empty house by people watching while sitting on a comfortable couch in the courtyard of a beautiful mall.

11   Don't make any major decisions, if you can help it, while in first grief. In fact, Verna Skinner, mentioned in number 7 above, has four don'ts for new widows. "Don't get married again the first year. Don't sell your house in the first year. Don't put all your money in one place. Don't give your money to your kids in the first year."

12   If you are lucky enough to have siblings, turn to them. Many women remember scrapping with their brothers and sisters when they were young and, then, not spending much time with them after marrying and being busy with a family of procreation. In old age, and especially after widowhood, some women have rediscovered their siblings, especially when siblings are also now alone. Two sisters who came to my Regis College Elderhostel rediscovered each other, so to speak, when both became widowed. Now in their seventies, they live together which is helpful financially and for security. Only one drives, so the other greatly benefits from this, but she is a more enthusiastic cook than her sister so she reciprocates by doing the cooking.

13   One widow learned how to manage her friends who, at first, either prattled on to entertain her and gave her a headache or else would not let her talk about her husband. They refused to do so themselves even though they had known him. She told them, "You don't have to distract me, and we can talk about Jim. He existed. It is good to talk about him." Soon she found her friends did not stop as if they had pulled a faux pas if they mentioned Jim, and eventually they were all able to share reminiscences of things they did when Jim was around. She also reported that she told family and friends who thought that in six months she should be all healed, that "it takes longer. Read the literature, and you'll see I am not abnormal."

14   Consider getting a pet if you live alone and don't plan to travel much.

15   Think of widowhood as sad but also the beginning of the rest of your life, as Dr. Silverman says.

16   Turn to God and/or to your sense of the continuity of life and meaning even when individuals die.

In my poetic drama, *Button, Button, Who Has the Button?*, an eighty-two year old widow says:

No love is lost
even though the lover
turns away from us
or life.

Within us are the people
we have loved,
not as they were
but as we wanted
them to be.

As our fresh grief
softens to sorrow,
we suddenly discover
the lover's eyes
in our mirror

the lover's words
on our lips,
even the beloved's jokes
have become ours.

What reality has taken,
we have taken
for our own.
Nothing is ever lost.
Layers of our being
contain all that has
lived for us
or that we imagined.

We exude
the strength
of our losses
and our gains glow
even in the dark.

Whether you have lost a spouse or a child, another relative or a friend, you have a right to your pain and rage. There will always be scars, but I hope you, too, will exude strength eventually and gain in your capacity for understanding the pain of others and your capacity for growth.

*
* *

Readings on Bereavement and Widow's Issues

This is only a sample. You will find many other books in libraries and stores. "On Being Alone": free pamphlet in English or Spanish, Fulfillment, AARP 1909 K Street, Northwest, Washington, D.C. 20049. This excellent booklet has a bibliography.

The Widow's Handbook: A Guide for Living, Charlotte Foehner and Carol Cozart, Fulcrum Inc., Golden, Colorado, 1988.

Helping Women Cope With Grief, Phyllis R. Silverman, Sage Publishing, Beverly Hills, CA, 1980.

Widow to Widow, Phyllis Silverman, Springer Publishing Co., New York, 1986.

Mutual Help Groups: Organization and Development, Phyllis Silverman, Sage Publishing Co., Beverly Hills, CA, 1981.

Living When a Loved One Has Died, Earl A. Grollman, Beacon Press, Boston, MA, 1987.

When Bad Things Happen to Good People, Harold Kushner, Schocken Books, New York, 1981.

Biopsychosocial Aspect of Bereavement edited by Sidney Zisook, M.D., American Psychiatry Press, Washington, D.C., 1987.

CHAPTER SEVENTEEN

Paid Work

CONGRATULATIONS if you are gain-
fully employed and like your job. In that case, you probably do not
need this chapter. You have a right, legally and otherwise, to keep working as long as you like. If you do not like your job, this chapter may
give you some ideas. If you are looking for work, this chapter may also
be useful.

Lots of older women love their jobs and thrive on them and are
greatly appreciated. Many old women do not like their jobs because
they are not valued by employers and fellow employees. They are
underpaid, exploited, overworked and their experience, skills, and
judgement not utilized. Ageism and sexism are real. Financial constraints may make it necessary for you to put up with this, or you may
be able to change yourself or the situation.

Again, the trouble may be that you do not have enough self-
confidence or self-respect to ask for more money or more consideration. You may be afraid to assert yourself. You may think you always
have to meet others needs, as many women do. You may need a big
sister like me to tell you that you are not everybody's mother, having
to nurture everyone at work.

Older women tend to do more than everyone. They do their bosses'
work as well as their own. They clean up after everyone and cover up
for them. They do a lot of free social work helping fellow employees
in many ways, personal and professional. Then they wonder why they
are so tired. They think, "Oh, I am getting old" rather than, "I am
doing too much." Think about it.

Older women also are prone to guilt. They take work home and worry about work more than do people socialized in more entitled eras. They work overtime without asking for compensation. If they have expense accounts, they keep them low so that everyone will think, "Oh, what a good girl."

They think the world is fair—that everyone will notice how hard they work and that rewards will be forthcoming. They do not tell people about their accomplishments, and they report their failures. Well, it is not a fair world, and nobody is noticing how hard you work *or* your success. You have to make sure people know your accomplishments, and you better learn to keep quiet about your failures.

Look at the young men in your workplace. Mostly they are advancing their own careers while you are helping them and everyone else, not working on your own advancement and well being. Probably, you were brought up to do this in human relationships and get satisfaction out of helping others. Okay, if this keeps you happy, keep up this style of worklife. But, if underneath you are resentful, brooding, depressed, angry, full of rage, well, it is time to be Out Rage Ous. Throughout this book, you have had lots of tips about being assertive and creative in changing yourself and situations. Work on it.

Above all, don't be grateful that they keep you around at your age. You have as much right to work as anyone, and you are more experienced and wiser at your age than younger people. You should be at the head of the class, not shrinking in the back. Be a proud tall tulip instead of a shrinking violet. Nobody really likes a martyr . . . it makes them uneasy. Besides, you burn out and are good to nobody, including yourself.

I have heard many old women brag that they never take a sick day. It is a matter of pride with them. It is also pretty stupid sometimes. You need a mental health day once in awhile, a day which I call a "me day," when you can do all the things you need to do for yourself like grooming, errands, and so forth. You also need, now and then, a "be day" when you can just be and stop pushing. Look around your workplace if you are a "gold star" never-absent, and see how others now and then take a day without censure. Are you a saint? Are you superwoman? Are you stupid?

Now, I am not asking you to be slothful or indifferent. It is just that practically all older women are over-conscientious and need to be told to pace themselves for the long haul at work. Some of them even might retire to enjoy life, and have the means to do so, but guilt, not job satisfaction, prevents retirement. They wonder how people would ever manage without them. More importantly, they wonder if they deserve to have leisure. They think they are only worthwhile if they are drudges. When such women do retire, they start doing for everybody through church work, volunteer work, or otherwise. It is so hard to do for themselves.

You might ask yourself, do you really *want* to keep working? Or are you afraid of retirement? If you are afraid of retirement, let me assure you that there is life after work. I was one who was anxious about giving up a full time job. I was unnecessarily anxious. Part time work, including writing, have been very satisfactory, and I enjoy not being structured all the time.

If you are not enjoying full time work, would you consider working part time and taking your social security? If you take it earlier than 65, you get somewhat less, but you get it for more years so it evens out. If you are over 65, you can still earn more than $9,000 a year and get full social security. After 70, you can earn as much as you want and get social security. The rules change now and then and so do the amounts you can earn. To get the latest data, call social security at its free number, 1-800-772-1213. There are excellent pamphlets available at your local social security office.

Like most women, you would probably benefit from taking a financial management seminar where you figure out what your assets and expenses are and how you would manage in retirement. Be careful of people who give these because they want to hard-sell you their financial products or services. Contact your regional or the national office of AARP to see where a women's financial planning seminar sponsored by AARP will be available. Or consider arranging one for your network. There are also good courses and workshops given by community colleges, councils on aging, religious groupings, and other sponsors. Many older women need help figuring out their finances.

When you stop working, some expenses go down, but others stay the same. Your travel and recreation costs may increase because you will have more free time. There is cheap recreation around though, and you should become an expert in ferreting it out.

Rhoda, who used to belong to an expensive health club, now swims at her town's high school pool during senior citizen hours and enjoys this as much. Sara, who used to pay high prices for evening and weekend movies, now goes to the bargain matinees. Rose borrows library books instead of buying books.

All this may seem trivial to you. You may have lost your job, or suddenly, after not having worked outside the home, you want to go to work for money, or structure and a feeling of importance, or to use your skills. How do you go about getting a job in a tough and ageist job market?

Here are some suggestions.

1 If it is in the area, use the placement office of the college or other school you attended. You are entitled to lifetime service. Make an appointment with a counselor there. If your educational institution or institutions are in another part of the country, this is not feasible unless you are open to relocating. But you can write about your plight and ask for any free job literature they have. They will usually send you stuff on how to write a resumé and how to behave in an interview. That is useful stuff. Sometimes, for a fee, you can be served at a college placement office even though you are not an alum. For example, Radcliffe Career Services, in Cambridge, MA, has a fee-for-service arrangement and a special interest in older women. I served on an advisory committee for a series of public lectures Radcliffe held for older women seeking paid work.

2 Tell everyone you know, even unlikely people, you are looking for a job. You never know who will hear about something and relay it. Most jobs are gotten through such informal contacts.

3 Use your state employment services, private agencies where employers pay the fees, and special agencies set up for women or for older people. They exist in many metropolitan areas. In Boston, OPERATION ABLE and the Jewish Vocational Service, for example, are especially geared to help older people of all religions. Several years ago, Dr. Paula Rayman of the Stone Center, Wellesley College, started, with others, to run groups for older women looking for work. These sup-

port groups were enabling. Eventually, Paula and others were able to set up the Advocacy Center for Women in Newton, Mass., which was housed in the basement of a church and open to all. There are open evenings, support groups for women seeking work, and other programs. You might consider helping found such a center in your area if one does not exist. Get information from the Advocacy Center for Women to use as a model. (Address: Advocacy Center for Older (40+) Women Workers, 474 Center Street, Newton, MA 02158, Phone (617) 244-3304.

3 Read newspaper advertisements faithfully, and respond immediately to those in which you are interested. Don't get depressed if you don't hear from employers. Some of them get so many responses, they are not polite about answering. Keep trying.

4 If you are getting no responses at all, rethink your goals for the type of job, rewrite your resume, get help from a counselor. Also think about some of the suggestions below.

5 Perhaps you can offer a service instead of getting a job. A mature woman in my area decided to start a livery service. She drives people to the airport and picks them up. I use her all the time because she is dependable, good company, and charges less than the cabs. But she does have to carry livery insurance and get up early in the morning to catch planes. Think of the pros and cons of any service you offer.

A 68 year old woman has put together three part time jobs which works out well for her. She serves one night a week as paid secretary to the selectmen in her town, types up the minutes, and sends them to the selectmen before the next meeting. She teaches Yoga in her home to several classes. She works on Saturdays in a clothing store and enjoys getting a discount on purchases of clothes for herself and for gifts.

Which talents, hobbies, and skills have you that you could get paid for? Some women have alterations businesses which they enjoy because they like to sew. A splendid cook caters small parties in peoples' homes. A green thumber is paid by local banks, stores, and businesses to come in and care for their plants. A former nurse who can no longer do the hard work of nursing now works for a florist making flower arrangements.

She says, "In all my years working in hospitals, I surely got to see a lot of flower arrangements, and I love knowing that some of the ones I make now go to cheer people up. Besides, in the florist shop, when the flowers die, we just throw them out. We don't have to deal with what went wrong or with grief stricken relatives."

6 If you are wanting to work part time, try to figure out the businesses or services in your community that have certain peak hours and offer your services for those hours.

7 Keep flexible. Don't let your pride stand in the way of earning. You may have had a high powered, prestigeful job earlier in life, but now you might, like the nurse described above, enjoy an easier job.

8 When job seeking, keep a notebook of contacts, places to call back, leads people give you. You can get so busy looking for a job that you can forget what you did or have to do. Don't put stuff on little scraps of paper that you will lose.

9 Consider working for a temporary agency. I know retired teachers who have done this. They loved the variety of ADULTS in different settings they met this way.

10 Consider being a substitute teacher if you have a college degree. I did this the first year I stopped being a college professor full time. It gave me a chance to be with young children and see what was going on in the public schools in several systems. Later, I went to part time teaching in colleges, but I do not regret the time spent substitute teaching. The hours were short, the pay reasonable, and the learning was great.

11 Use your public library to read books on how to get jobs, how to start a small business, etc.

12 Consider taking a course or some short or long term training for a job. I cannot advise you about areas because that depends on your interests and what educational facilities exist where you live. Explore

yourself, and explore educational opportunities. Do not think you are too old to learn. You are not.

13   When you go to a job interview, dress as you would for that kind of job. Go light on jewelry and makeup unless you are applying for a job in the fashion industry.

14   In the interview, focus on the employers' needs and wants, not yours. The employer wants to know what you can for the employer, not what the employer can do for you. But be sure to describe volunteer work in which you have exercised skills and talents that can help the employer. Also, be sure to point out that your home management skills can be utilized, if appropriate. There is a carryover from the skills of running a home and caring for children to the skills in many jobs. Translate your volunteer and homemaking achievements into skills for your resumé. For example, you have skills budgeting, coordinating, supervising people, organizing.

15   Consider that a stipended semi-volunteer job like Foster Grandparents might give you a little money and the structure you need. Or consider unpaid volunteer work to get experience, entry, references, and satisfaction.

16   Browse in the yellow pages of your phone book for ideas about places you might work. Also, if there is a United Fund in your community for charitable organizations and social agencies, get the list and description of what these agencies do from the Fund. Perhaps you could get a job with one.

17   Check with your local senior center to see if there are job listings for older people.

18   Use the telephone when feasible, but go out and let people see how great you are in person.

19   Advertise your services in the local papers and on bulletin boards.

20   Hospitals and hotels work around the clock. Consider the evening or late night shift. Institutions for the elderly, the mentally ill, exceptional children, the severely handicapped, often have trouble getting

and keeping good help. If you have a lot of love to give, those are places it is badly needed.

21   If your area has no jobs, consider re-locating to someplace where there are jobs, but weigh this carefully. Take a trial visit. Look before you burn your bridges.

22   If you can't get a job and have no money, don't let your pride stand in the way of applying for help at government and private agencies. You deserve.

23   Consider, perhaps with other older women, getting a grant to create a program to help older people and create jobs for you and others. Talk to folks at your state and municipal departments of elder affairs.

24   Hook up with some people who can hear your horror stories of the job search, give you feedback, and keep telling you how great you are.

25   Keep up your nutrition, other health care, and exercise while you are looking for a job. Take periods of relaxation. If you are totally stressed, nobody is likely to hire you.

26   Take an entry level job even if you are much more highly qualified. Getting your foot in the door is important. Once you are in, maybe a more challenging opening will occur, and you will be on the spot. You can also enlarge your job once you are in. Also be realistic about what you can get in a tough job market with the ageism in the society. Recently, I met a bright, well educated woman who is working at MacDonald's and really loves it. She enjoys the adolescents who work there, and she likes watching the customers. She doesn't take the work home with her, and she gets a free meal during her shift. Another woman I know is enthusiastic about working in the frozen yogurt shop where sooner or later she has a chance to chat with everyone she knows.

27   If you like homemaking and taking care of others, consider work- ing for a dual career young family or working as a homemaker or home

health aide for frail elders. You can work for individuals or work through agencies.

28 Babysitting pays very well now.

29 If you experience rejection, try to realize it is not you. It is the job market.

30 Don't be afraid of high tech. You can learn. Also think about non-traditional work which pays more than so-called women's jobs. These days women work in so-called dirty jobs. You can always take a bubble bath afterwards if you get dirty at work.

31 Above all, stay away from the Mr. Klutz type. (See chapter six.)

32 If you have some other ideas, share them with me so I can add them to future editions of this book. Get ideas from all the women you know, especially those who are working. Keep up your courage.

CHAPTER EIGHTEEN

Alphabet for Economizing

WE OLDER WOMEN generally don't have much money so we have to think creatively about how to economize and stretch our funds. When I was swimming laps at the pool, my most relaxed state, it occurred to me that I ought to provide you with a listing of ways to save money. I decided to do this in an alphabet. I enjoyed reading alphabet books when I was a child, and, later, I liked reading them to my children. I was writing the alphabet for older women's economies while I was drying and asked the help of seasoned citizen swimmer, Carolyn Cameron, so this alphabet is a collaboration with her.

A is for Ask. If you encounter something you would like to do but it is too expensive, ask if there are special financial arrangements for seasoned citizens, people on limited fixed income, or, if you are not yet age 65, for low-income older women. It doesn't hurt to ask. It often works out that people are glad to have you for what you can pay. For example, I wanted to attend a writers' conference I couldn't afford, said so, and was offered a greatly reduced rate. For the International Women's Writing Guild conference I did pay full rate, having more money at the time, but there were other older women there who bartered their services by running workshops or working at the registration and information desks. Many therapists have sliding scales, but they don't know you are at the lower end unless you point it out. Theaters will sometimes give you free admission to concerts or non-equity plays in return for ushering, helping with the sale of drinks at intermission, etc. Non profit conference and retreat centers also allow you to barter help or give you reduced rates. I have found even stores, especially small ones, will reduce merchandise for you and are glad to make the sale. People may refuse when you ask, but you can handle that.

B is for Bottles. In most states, there is a deposit return on cans of tonic and bottles of beer. Yet people throw these along roads at beaches and elsewhere. Don't have false pride. Pick them up. I do when I walk, partly for environmental cleanliness and recycling. But it was nice to get a $1 or so worth of bottles every day. Multiplying it by 365 is the money for a vacation air ticket or some other goodie.

C is for Cafeterias. When you travel, or if you live in a college town, use the college cafeterias. The food is much cheaper than anywhere else, and there are usually great self service salad bars. Once you pay, you can usually have all you want. No tipping. The best part is you can talk with the students and keep in touch with that generation. Another bonus is that entries to most college cafeterias are filled with posters announcing events at the college. These are usually free and often wonderful. If you are a tourist, you can also get tips from students on places to see, places to shop, public transportation, and all the inexpensive entertainment around. Students who generally don't have much money either are expert at this.

D is for Discount. I have been with women my age and older who refuse to use senior citizen identity cards to get senior citizen discounts. They suffer from inward ageism. They refuse to reveal their ages to the senior centers or other places which provide these cards. Actually, they suffer only in the pocketbook since people can probably guess their ages anyway. Most municipal councils of aging provide a list of businesses that give senior discounts, and merchants are pleased to have your business. Always ask if there is a senior discount before the sale is rung up, not after. Some beauty parlors have special senior citizen hours or day. Not only do you save money, but you get a chance to meet age peers and maybe make new friends. If you are not yet a senior citizen, you have something to look forward to when you grow up. The price of movies these days makes the senior discount a big help. Airlines, AMTRAK, and many businesses also give senior citizen discounts, and some also have special tickets you can buy for unlimited or frequent travel.

E is for Early Bird. Many restaurants have very inexpensive early bird meals if you eat early in the evening. Check these specials out.

F is for the Family Size. Many stores sell large packages of poultry, hamburg, or produce for a much lower price per pound. If you have a freezer, buy these large sizes and divide them, or find friends or neighbors who will split packages with you. Just because you are single, doesn't mean you have to lose bargains. And make your own TV dinners by preparing larger quantities and freezing portions.

G is for Gifts. Instead of spending more money than you can afford on gifts, give simple ones, or, cheaper and better still, offer loving services to people as a gift. If you drive, you could do an errand for someone, transport that person to the airport, etc. You could plant for a woman with a bad back who likes flowers.

H is for Haircuts. If the beauty parlor is too expensive, see if there is a beauty school near you. Students need people to practice on, and the students are usually good and eager to please. You can also get luxuries like manicures at these schools.

I is for Investigate. Don't make any major purchases or investments without doing research in *Consumer Reports*, among friends, and elsewhere.

J is for Jewelry. Sell stuff you will never wear again at consignment shops. Why decorate drawers? Senior citizens in Framingham, MA, have a shop called the Heritage Gallery where they also sell their dishes, glasses, bric-a-brac, clothes. Start one if there is none in your area.

K is for Kindness. If you can't afford to give to charities financially, start giving services to people. One woman on a very limited budget, allocates twenty-five cents a day to charity. During her daily walk, she finds a car parked at an expired meter and puts in the quarter to save someone a $10 fine. It makes her feel great to confer this favor on strangers. Another woman who could not even afford the twenty-five cents a day makes a cheery telephone call every day to a shut-in.

L is for Long Distance. Stop spending money you can't afford to call long distance to people whose voices you don't really need to hear. Instead, buy a stack of postcards at the post office and use these. Even if your descendants live at a distance, letters can be a good form of communication. You can express yourself thoughtfully and at length in a letter for the cost of one stamp. Writing can also convey a sense of your personality, style, and life that a hurried phone call with an eye on the clock may not. Letters may also be treasured by your descendants years from now. Letters may be shared with more than one person by your xeroxing or by those who receive them.

M is for Mix. Mix your own salad dressings out of things like mayo, vinegar, yogurt, herbs, and spices. This is much cheaper than buying them, and it is fun to experiment with outrageous concoctions. Hint: Put it in a bottle with a ribbon around it and a label (My Special Dressing). These make great inexpensive gifts. There are lots of other kinds of foods you can mix up yourself for less cost than bought mixes. One friend mixes all kinds of soup beans in colorful packets, puts in herbs and spices, packages them in plastic baggies, and has cheap but useful soup mix Christmas presents to tie with a piece of red yarn (that is much cheaper than ribbon).

N is for New. Things don't have to be new. I have already lobbied in this book for thrift shops and garage sales where you can get great gently used items. Your imagination can help. I bought a beat up broom in a yard sale for a dime, keep it in my car in the winter, and for short me it is great for sweeping the snow off my car roof and sides. I also have stopped spending three dollars for de-icer in spray cans to do my side and rear window. I used an old manual spray bottle filled with the inexpensive windshield washer that comes cheap in gallons to put in your car windshield washer storage tank.

O is for Organizations. Units of belongingness are great if you utilize them. But you may be paying dues out of habit to organizations in which you have lost interest, or you may not have asked if they have retirees' or older person's rates.

P is for Prescriptions. You may be able to get generics for less if your physician approves, or you may be able to save by going to a store that give a discount, or you may want to use a mail order service like AARP's.

Q is for Quit. Quit buying on impulse items you don't need including items in glossy catalogues on which you have to pay mailing charges, unless you are housebound or in a rural area. You can often get these items cheaper at a discount store.

R is for Refrain. Refrain from using your credit card to buy more than you can afford, especially if you will have to let the bill ride and pay large interest charges. But if you *do* use credit cards, refrain from writing checks or mailing them too early so that you will lose interest on the money in your bank account. Refrain also, if you have grandchildren, from giving them more than you can afford. Let them love you for yourself, not for your presents.

S is for Shampoo. Most shampoo bottles are designed in such a way that too much pours out. Save an old bottle, and split the new bottle into two by pouring half over and adding water. This is also better for your hair. The diluted shampoo is less drying, and our hair is dry at older ages.

T is for Tea Bags. Three herb tea bags in an interesting flavor makes a quart of great iced refresher, far cheaper than bottled drinks you buy and better for you than sugary ones. T could also be for trade in your gas guzzling car for a more energy-efficient one.

U is for Underwear which, if no one sees it, is fine to wear when shabby. Handwashing it preserves it for much longer than using the washer.

V is for Vegetables. Always check the area where most supermarkets put vegetables and fruit that may have minor defects. Often, the only reason the produce is there is because it is already ripe. Ripe fruit and vegetables are great. You can eat much healthier if you have lots of fresh fruits and vegetables; you can save much money by going for the "distressed ones." When my store hasn't wheeled out the shelves that have such produce, I ask. They let me into the back room where the stuff is being accumulated on the portable shelves. A much enjoyed contribution to a potluck is a great fruit salad you make out of wonderful ripe fruit at cut-rate prices from this source. You cut away any blemishes when you make the fruit salad.

W is for Wash and Wear. A wash and wear haircut means no expensive trips to the beauty shop. Wash and wear clothes mean no dry cleaning bills. You can wash raincoats and lots of other things if you are careful.

X is for Xerox. One of the best gifts I got on my 65th birthday was from my friend Carmen Ward who xeroxed some poems and other things she thought I would like. This is much better and more personal than an expensive printed card or some bought thing I might not need.

Y is for Yarn. If you are a knitter, rip up old stuff you no longer use and reuse the yarn. Or buy knitted stuff cheap at rummage sales and rip them apart for the yarn. Use old bits of yarn instead of ribbon.

Z is for Zipper. You, too, can salvage an old one and sew it in for a broken zipper instead of taking a garment to a fix-it shop where it will sit for a month and be repaired expensively. I, who don't sew, discovered it was easier than I thought.

My alphabet is done but these are not the only ways to save. They are simply ideas to get you started thinking creatively, and even outrageously, about what you can substitute, do without, or invent. We really have to use our heads when our pocketbooks are lean. Sometimes we just don't think. I realized this one day when I was in a large office building attending a meeting with about 100 other older women. At the coffee break, practically all of us ran to the two-stall bathroom on the floor, and there was a tremendous line. Some women muttered about liberating the men's room. That would have been easy as women could have taken turns watching outside. But there was a simpler solution. I figured out there must be a bathroom on every floor of the building and simply popped into the elevator, went down a floor, and had a bathroom all to myself. When I finished, I went back in the spirit of sisterhood and told those still waiting in line to go spread out on the other floors. They did, and several said, "Why didn't I think of that?"

They didn't think of it because we all get into a rut as well as lines.

Look at the things you do and the products and services you use, and make some new contributions to your finances and my alphabet.

I went along for years paying top prices for the cookies I brought, nurturer that I am, to my classes and workshops. All those years, on my regular route I passed a bakery thrift shop. Somehow, I thought it would be cheating folks to get the stuff there. Finally, I went in, and discovered it had exactly the same brand of cookies at half the price I had been paying. People enjoyed the cookies just as much, and I saved good money.

Now you may be a rich leader and not have needed these hints. Great. One person who previewed this laughed and said C should be for Checks she wrote against her husband's account. Even though he was a nuisance, she put up with the marriage so she would have plenty of money. We can all choose.

These hints may also represent triviality to women who do not have enough money to survive, to pay rent, to buy food and medications. In that case, chapter eight may have been helpful to you regarding housing alternatives. For most people, housing is the biggest expense. Also, be sure to check whether you are eligible for food stamps, and get them. They are no disgrace. You can check this out at your aging or social security office. And see if you are eligible for S.S.I. or for general relief. Many cities and towns distribute surplus food and have food pantries for free food. There are also free meals provided at some churches and food centers. Find out from your local social agencies about these.

CHAPTER NINETEEN

Benefits of Aging

AGING has a bad press. People tend to see the negative aspects, forgetting the good things aging brings. They see aging as signaling the end of life, forgetting that with today's longevity, people, especially women, will live longer as old people than they did as youths. When I tell my twenty year old students that they will be old persons longer than they have already lived, they think I am crazy because they think they have already lived forever. If you consider the official age of being old as 65, most of us will be old for decades.

The old are often divided into three groups, the young old from 65 to 75 or the go goes, the old from 75 to 85 or the slow goes, and the very old from 85 up or the no goes. These, of course, are stereotypes. There are many vigorous people at the far end of the chronological scale, and many young people in their twenties who are no goes, being lazy or blocked.

Retirees are living much longer these days and enjoying good activities as I have been pointing out in this book. After life times of working and caring for others, they have time for themselves.

Six months after I retired, I realized how boxed-in I had been in my job. I prepared a new kind of box, a poem in the shape of one.

Retirement
Progress Report

The curse of duty lifted
my priorities are sifted
and emphasis has shifted

from doing what is right
for everyone in my sight
to seeking out the light
of what Ruth wants to be
and who she wants to see
in time still left to me.

It was fun writing that box poem and having the time to do it one fine morning instead of getting on the Massachusetts Turnpike, a hectic road, to drive an hour to work. Since I wrote the poem, my priorities have continued to shift toward figuring out what I want to do rather than what I must do. Other retirees report a similar sense of freedom, and even euphoria.

There is time to look around you, discovering that you don't really need a lot of material things and can get pleasure from simple things. In our younger years, many of us are driven my ambition or the desire to keep up with the Joneses. We have come, in our later years, to see that even if the Joneses have more, this is not necessarily the route to contentment for them. You might consider a little poem I wrote called Competition because the poem is a metaphor for living simply and liking it.

All my neighbors have fancy feeders
and bright flowers to lure the birds.
I throw seed on my barren porch rail.
The birds adore and adorn my neighbors
but when these busy gardeners clatter
and call loudly across their yards
"my anemones are prettier then yours"
the birds
        s c   t t e
           a   r
sneaking a little peace and snack
at my no frills luncheonette
twisting their heads to make sure
no one sees them slumming
tipping with a trill or two.

When we get old, we can lower our standards for ourselves and laugh about ourselves, not be so hard on ourselves. I used to berate myself for my poor housekeeping. Now I have mellowed.

> I catalogue my secret sins
> and some quite obvious
> like my messy self and home.
> But the mouse in my house
> thinks me kind with crumbs
> and the spiders love me
> for not cleaning corners.

Most old women I know are also able to enjoy the perks of aging and have a sense of humor about themselves and their discomforts. The women in my town of Wellesley Senior Citizen poetry writing group wrote a group poem in which each woman did one line to finish the sentence starting Aging is. This is their poem.

What Is Aging?

Aging is:
The orange time of life, vivid, hopeful
wrinkling, sprinkling, winkling,
fierce attention and careful monitoring,
getting older, hopefully becoming wiser
and enjoying each day as it comes—
savoring life. Aging is full measure,
learning to live for today and tomorrow,
being thankful for every single day.

Aging is:
sometimes a slide, sometimes a climb,
coming to the last lines of the melody of life,
amalgamating memories happy, sad, useful
climbing stairs one at a time,
a pain in every joint,
adaptability to change

without feeling its losses,
a great opportunity to develop courage.

Aging is:
Too soon old, too late smart,
another blessed open door,
growing better while growing older,
enjoying a wonderful life
continuing to unfold,
looking forward to tomorrow,
a time to reminisce
and do the things you missed.

Aging is:
The small mysteries—
What happened to my keys, eyeglasses, letters
and the kind voice that says "Let's help each other."
Aging is what happens to my body while
my inner child stays always young and beautiful.
Aging is delightful and enlightening,
learning I can change as I get older, never OLD.
Aging is a kaleidoscope of bright colors
becoming softer, sweeter but right to the point
and finding out with surprise and delight
that I will never come to the end of my self.

Now these were all women who had enough money to live on. Being poverty stricken when old is another matter, and one we should all try to remedy. However, there is less poverty now among the old since we have social security indexed to inflation and at least inadequate S.S.I. for people not eligible for social security. We need to do more to get funds for the poor old and better health coverage for the old, but Medicare is a big help even though it doesn't cover everything. Those who need nursing home care and do not have funds can be covered by Medicaid, but those above the allowable income for Medicaid must spend down to be eligible for it. Certainly there are losses and decrements in old age.

This chapter, however, is about the benefits so let me list some more. A nice bonus is that you are allowed eccentric and outrageous behavior. Many people liked Jenny Joseph's title poem in the book *When I Am an Old Woman I Will Wear Purple*, (edited by Sandra Martz, Papier Mache Press, Watsonville, CA, 1988). They resonated to the idea that old women had the license to stop being "ladies" and start acting out. We have to repress and suppress a lot during much of our life. Old age brings a certain freedom. We can live out some of our fantasies. More important, however, is that old age brings wisdom. You see what is really vital and what is trivial. You can value people because they amuse or interest you rather than because they can help you advance or because you have obligations to them. You can paint for the pleasure of painting, not for the approval of others, for instance.

Being a long liver is also greater than the alternative. The joy is that you get to see your descendants and other younger people develop and grow. You can also watch history. You have a good sense of history because you have lived long. What is text book knowledge for the young, you saw first hand. You can pass on your knowledge. Also, in the course of your life you have learned a lot of jokes, and now you can tell them. Many schools utilize seasoned citizens to share oral history and fun with students. More should.

It is true, a small percentage of old people suffer such diseases as Alzheimer, but the chances of that happening to you are not enormous. Young people have illnesses, too. We do have frailties and loss of sensory acuity as time goes on, but there are now good aids like hearing devices, optical surgery improvements, physical therapy. If you are newly old, don't brood about what may happen in the future. Enjoy the present, and make intelligent plans to keep as well and active as possible in the future.

Some of the depression associated with certain aged people is due to environmental conditions and lack of stimulation. Work to give yourself the best possible environment, perhaps using some of the suggestions in the book. Also, don't let yourself get bored; then you won't be depressed or boring.

Life after youth can be a good phase of life. Summon your courage and skills and humor to make it so. With a little help from your friends, you should be fine. Use resources and use your good sense and experience.

Graduation and Commencement

BY NOW, you are on your way to being an outrageous woman – or to rejecting the whole idea and wondering why you bothered to read this book. I hope you are recruited to outrageousness. If so, I would like to say goodbye with a graduation ceremony. This ceremony starts with a grey haired, beautiful valedictorian whose commencement speech is:

"I own my years. I am proud to be a long liver and to associate with other long livers. Rather than asking them, how old are you, I will ask them how many years have you lived? There is a difference in the two questions because how old are you is passive. How many years have you lived implies accomplishments. It is an accomplishment to be an old woman, especially considering the amount of sexism and ageism in the stressful society.

"I intend to be outrageous for the rest of my life. Being outrageous means that I will not accept insults, being ignored, or being maltreated. I deserve to be valued, listened to, and respected and treated well by others. I also deserve to listen to my own needs and wants and to try to fulfill them.

"I will be outrageous also in the pursuit of a good society and world for all people, young, middle aged, and old. I will use my crone's wisdom to nag, advocate, fight for good causes, and fight against the bad.

"I consider myself and other old women beautiful. Our face wrinkles record the wonderful emotions we have expressed all our lives and will continue to express. Our bodies also show the burdens we have carried and the wonderful journeys we have made. Our grey or white hair is a halo softening our features and symbolizing our new beauty. I will be vital in my dress, not drab as if to hide myself. I am not a bit of refuse from life. I am a celebration of it."

After the valedictorian speaks, each member of the graduating class makes her vows. You, having read this book, are a member of the graduating class. Right now, while your mind is on it, write down the general attitude you will have as you grow older and the specific actions or activities you would like to take. Make yourself some plans and promises about how you will be outrageous. After you have written your graduation remarks, hang them on your refrigerator or bulletin board so that you will be reinforced in your outrageousness by your own words.

Also, share what you have written with people you know. If you care to share them with me, you can send them to me at my home, 75 High Ledge Avenue, Wellesley, MA 02181. I would love to read them.

Finishing this book is a graduation for me too. I have wanted to write this book for a long time. But, as commencement speakers always say, graduation is only the start. At 70, I have yet to learn how to be seventy and, with any luck, eighty and ninety. Whatever your age, you too have a future in which you will get even older. So let us seek out women older than ourselves, celebrate them and learn from them. If they need help, maybe we can help them also, setting a pattern for when we might need help ourselves.

May you have courage and joy in your older womanhood. Enjoy your wisdom and share it. Laugh as much as you can. Cry when you must.

Here are poems celebrating being seventy and eighty. If you are not that age yet, you do have something to look forward to. The poems are from *Button, Button, Who has the Button?* my poetic drama cited earlier.

Seventy

Seventy is being outside
on a November day
knowing the fragility
of sunshine.

Seventy is facing lost causes
and fighting on
having little to lose.

Seventy is loss
and dry tears unseen
but also passion
and private jokes
suddenly revealed by life.

Seventy is waking early
to seek treasures
which there is no room
to hold.

Seventy is sensing
which stranger
will give the ecstasy
of friendship
and who will betray.

At seventy
you grasp wisdom
in your hands
while they
are still strong.

Go into seventy
hoping and loving
you will be women
made beautiful
by having lived
well and long.

Eighty-Two

Two years past eighty
I forget a lot of things
I don't want to remember
like watching my words.
I remember a lot of things
I thought I had forgotten
like Miss Brown
who made kindergarten
another home.

Two years past eighty
I own my old body
with all its imperfections
and like myself.

Two years past eighty
I spot a new bird
learn a wildflower's name
see a great grandchild smile
hear live, for the first time,
Bach's Sonata in C Major,
tell the President off,
drink a new wine,
and make new friends
of you.

Post Graduation

AFTER SEVERAL reprintings of the first edition of this book (KIT, Inc., 1991), I now have the privilege of providing this postgraduate chapter for the second edition. It is time to tell what I have learned from the questions and comments of the many women who, having "graduated," called me or wrote to me.

Hundreds of women have been kind enough to tell me the book has changed their lives for the better, making them more outrageous and giving them new directions. It has changed my life also because I have been invited to speak all over the country and have listened to the stories and problems of women in training to be R.A.S.P.s. Women from foreign countries have come to the workshops. One women from Australia, for example, told me she had worn out her copy, lending it to friends. Older women's issues transcend nationality.

Women everywhere are wearing the "I am An Outrageous Older Woman" and "R.A.S.P" buttons, carrying R.A.S.P. tote bags and wearing the tee shirts that say "Outrageous Older Women" (Available through KIT, Inc., Publishers.) I love it! We older women, as the largest aggregate of Americans, are beginning to substitute two positive P's, *Pride* and *Power,* for the negative P's that have undermined many older women. (See "Expanding Social Roles for Older Women" by Ruth Harriet Jacobs in *Women On the Front Lines, Meeting the Challenge of an Aging America*, edited by Jesse Allen and Alan Pifer, Urban Institute Press, New York, 1993.)

These are six negative P's.

Patriarchy - the systemic female subordination at work, at home, and in the structural arrangements of society.

Patterning - the pink blanket syndrome whereby socially acceptable behavior for women, especially older ones, is to conform to implicit rules that they be nurturing, non-sexual, self sacrificing, restrained, passive and modest.

Propriety - the expectation that women be dignified and accept narrow roles.

Politeness - the demand that women never show anger, always smile and say thank you even when they are ignored and insulted.

Perfectionism - the requirement that women do everything right for everybody and be neat while they perform. This immobilizes some women afraid to try because they might be seen as imperfect. (Inaction gets you nowhere.)

Pretty - the notion that women are only valuable if they are decorative and that older women are not valuable because they are not considered pretty.

Even young women are troubled by these P's. In fact, the twenty-year old student nurses in a sociology class at St. Elizabeth's Hospital, Boston, insisted upon adding "Pretty." They worried about what would happen when the beauty accolade passed to women younger than they.

At workshops, I have been asking older women to tell me about the outrageous things they have done. Their exploits have delighted me.

Seasoned women have fought age discrimination in the workplace, moved across the country, participated in public demonstrations, run for public office, written outrageous poems and letters, told off politicians, difficult husbands and children, started businesses late in life, taken adventure trips alone, and done many, many other things.

Mostly, they have raised their self-esteem and improved their public image. They have shed their internalized ageism and ventured new roles, picking themselves up and trying again if they failed. They have made new connections and created new groups. They have relieved themselves of anger and developed better identities.

Many have written for support or advice. To provide this, I have been writing hundreds of letters encouraging women and informing them of resources. One R.A.S.P., Joyce Cupps, decided to publish a bi-monthly magazine celebrating the return of the Crone. She named it *ENCORE.* Joyce was outrageous enough to ask me to write a column -

free - called "Outrageously Yours." It now appears regularly. (ENCORE is available from Joyce at 604 Pringle Avenue, Suite 91, Galt, CA 95632.)

The April 1993 column answered the question that has been most asked by readers who liked the descendant's chapter, especially the piece, "Why Older Mothers Have a Tough Time." I offer that column here.

Mother — From the Pedestal to the Trash?

Q. Dear Dr. Ruth: I am totally dismayed by the "mom trashing" going on in the U.S. with even therapists joining in and advising their clients to "divorce" their mothers. And have you seen the talk shows with moms being harangued by daughters in front of millions of people? The host and audience side with the daughters and interrupt the mothers so much they aren't even heard. I also have such a situation in my life, and I feel so many emotions I don't even know how to sort them out. I would like to know what you have to say about this problem that would help me and other older mothers deal with this. It causes many heartaches and disrupts family relationships.

A. I am very aware of this unfortunate trend. In fact, in my 1991 book, *Be an Outrageous Older Woman: A R.A.S.P.*, I wrote a one-page statement of "Why Older Mothers Can't Win" in the chapter on dealing with descendants. This page explained in detail how we are damned if we do and damned if we don't. It turns out that it is the most popular page in the book. A copy is hanging on many women's hall of fame — the kitchen refrigerator!

But mother blaming is not a new phenomena. Through American history, mothers have been blamed for the way the children turned out as if fathers or society had no impact; their progeny were simply sponges, not functioning humans in their own right.

What is new are two trends. First, folks like John Bradshaw, in videotapes and in writing, target parents as pathogenic. Other therapists who may have not worked through their own feelings about their parents encourage their clients to "divorce" their parents.

Secondly, life is hard today for young and middle-aged adults, and they look around for someone to blame for their unhappiness. To blame the bad state of society is abstract. To blame themselves is too painful. So, they feel that if somehow their parents had brought them up differently, they would be happier, stronger people.

The mother is more often blamed than the father because mother generally spent more time in the child rearing effort. And mothers were awfully good punching bags because as girls we were taught not to fight back and socialized to feel guilty about everything. Besides, the mother is usually a safe target for blame because she has unconditional love for her descendants and will not fight back for that reason.

I had a good illustration of this orgy of mother blaming two years ago at the annual daughter/mother day colloquium we sponsor at the Wellesley College Center for Research on Women. Hundreds of women come to this. That year, after the general session, we had break-out sessions on half a dozen topics. One session was on mothers and daughters and anger. Women were standing, sitting on the floor, crowded together while the other five sessions were practically empty. Daughters from 20 to 60 bitterly railed against what they thought their mothers had done to them or were doing, and not one woman complained about a daughter. Women even castigated mothers who were very old and already dead.

I sat there feeling sad and angry because I knew most of the mothers complained against had done the best they could and were perhaps culture victims themselves of bad societal or marital arrangements. It was then that I went home and wrote "Why Older Mothers Can't Win."

What I think the blamed mother needs to do is:

1. Realize this is a mass situation. You are one of many mothers being blamed.
2. Stop blaming yourself or accepting guilt. You did the best you could. You may not have been perfect, but nobody is.
3. Your adult daughter or son may be depressed because of societal issues or issues of their own making. Do not let them project societal inadequacies or their own inadequacies onto you.
4. Try writing a polite, understanding, but firm letter to your

son or daughter saying nobody is perfect, but you did the best you could and that you are suffering under this blaming and would like it stopped. Before mailing this letter, run it by some good friends to make sure you have not said something inappropriate in your anger and pain. Take their suggestions and rewrite it. Sometimes a short note is more effective than a long one that is too complicated.

5. Get your own therapist — someone who will support you and give you advice on how to withstand this abuse and how to respond. Social workers at Family Service agencies can be useful.

6. Ask around. You will find others in the same situation. Start a support group. In my town, one mother organized instead of agonized! She was broken-hearted after her daughter refused to see her. She formed a group M.E.S.C.H., Mothers of Estranged Children. The group filled quickly. Now there are groups in several other communities. You can start your own chapter of M.E.S.C.H. There are no dues and no rules. Just get together and support each other and exchange stories for dealing with this trauma. Announce your meeting on bulletin boards, or in local newspapers. It helps to tell your story in a confidential, emphatic atmosphere and to realize you are not a freak but one of many mothers trashed and targeted.

7. Write an unsent letter to your blaming descendant. By an unsent letter, I mean that you get your anger out in a reply to your nasty son or daughter and then tear up the letter. It is therapeutic.

8. Offer to go to therapy with your descendant and present your side of the story.

9. If your descendant is going to a bad therapist or a charlatan, and there are many, find a good one and recommend her. Offer to pay if you can afford it.

10. Pray and share your hurt with God and your clergy person who may offer you some comfort. He or she may even mediate if your descendant is willing.

11. If you have been trying to hold onto or control an adult child, desist immediately. Once our children are grown, they resent

interference. I prefer to call them descendants because "child" implies we still have a vote in their lives. And we do not.

12. This is perhaps most important. Have hope that things will change. Sometimes descendants cut the cord in painful ways but when they feel more like their own persons, they will return to a kinder, healthier, less dependent relationship. In fact, I know of many cases where descendants who have refused to see or be decent to mothers have later worked through their feelings and come around. In fact, the founder of the first M.E.S.C.H. chapter has observed this in the few years the group has been operating. One by one, there has been a healing. So take heart and take time.

You might be interested in a book telling the true story of how author Sylvia Grossman, late in her mother's life, made the leap to understanding and sympathy towards her mother. (*Making Peace With My Mother*, KIT Press, Manchester, CT., 1992, $14.95 paper.)

I also offer my mother and daughter readers this acrostic to consider.

Different Paths

D   ear mother, dear daughter
I   n certainty or uncertainty, you have
F   ollowed different paths passionately or petulantly
F   aithful to your own vision; blind to hers
E   stranged from each other
R   efusing perhaps, often despite pleading,
E   ven to address and consider
N   agging doubts and hurts
T   hat surge in your common, clotted blood.

P   erhaps I might entreat you
A   sk that you look beyond paths and pride
T   o the essence and pain of her who in all the world
H   as closest, oldest kinship to you
S   o hates but also loves the most.

(*Encore*, Vol. I, No. 4, 1993)

The second topic on which I have received considerable mail is sexuality. Some readers felt I should have included information on menopause. I didn't because there are already so many books on menopause. But for these women, I offer a poem in the voice of a thirty year old, a fifty year old, and a seventy year old. I am entitled to speak for a seventy year old because I am seventy. The poem has appeared in the *Journal of Women and Aging* in the issue on *Women and Healthy Aging*, but, if you are not a journal reader, here it is for you.(If you want to subscribe to this useful journal, it is published by the Haworth Press, 10 Alice Street, Binghampton, NY 13904-9981.)

Menopause

Thirty experiences
year after year
sisterhood of blood
accustomed rhythms
reassuring flow
inconvenient flow
disappointing flow
 I will not be
 like these old women
 I try not to see

Fifty inquires
when the blood ceases
what else will leave
when the blood dries
what else will dry
will the hot flashes
burn away desire
 will he leave me
 will I lose me
 what will old age be?

Seventy responds
we are not bloodless
we have new rhythms
our life force flows
love does not cease
desire does not dry
hot flashes of wit
     prove we are not lost
     we birth crone's wisdom
     see us hear our glee.

Some readers have inquired about gender differences in aging. So did the Boston Society for Gerontological Psychiatry which asked me to present on this topic at its November 1992 Scientific Meeting on Successful Aging. I decided to cut the boring review of literature by writing the differences in doggerel. I include it here because you may not be readers of the *Journal of Geriatric Psychiatry* in which it has appeared. (the Journal is published by International Universities Press, Inc., 59 Boston Post Road, Madison, CT 06443.)

His and Her Aging: A Review of the Literature

-1-
Both tend to retire gladly
but if forced out, leave madly.
Despite the myths, she like he,
misses colleagues she would see.
Retiring, she continues other roles.
His day has holes, lacks goals.
She more easily turns the page.
He is more often mired in rage.

-2-
Without erection, he has dejection
she usually settles for affection.
Her vaginal dryness yields to creams

but his impotence leads to screams.
She can remain orgasmic forever;
meds or surgery his potency can sever.
His prostate makes it hard to void;
her leakage makes her feel destroyed.

-3-
The blaming dysfunctional family fad
makes them both really sad
but adult children target more on hers.
He parented so little, no wrath incurs.
She broods on imagined guilt.
Children's criticism makes her wilt.
Yet suppressed incest charges rear
that in old age he may have to hear.

-4-
He can make the car run right.
Mechanically, she's not too bright.
He was taught to be a fixer;
she was taught to be a mixer.
A woman alone knows how to cook.
Most men alone need a cookbook.
He often manages their finances;
she's afraid of investment chances.

-5-
Ageism insults and hurts her more
at stages he continues to score.
Odd, she is labeled old quicker
but he dies sooner, sicker.
Though he doesn't live as long,
she may sing the martyr song.
Even when old, she caretakes others
much more than do her brothers.

-6-

She has less insurance, pension, cash
but knows how to concoct cheap hash.
Despite my attempt to be witty,
her old age poverty isn't pretty.
Very old, she has ample gender peers.
He is a minority in later years.
Strange in view of this configuration
Old men, not women, usually lead the nation.

-7-

She admits readily to depression;
he won't make this confession.
She sees more docs, downs more pills
but his stoicism and denial kills.
Her complaints doctors abhor;
his are attended to more.
Her symptoms are just post menopause
with him, docs look for a cause.

-8-

His dead wife was significant other;
he can feel like he lost his mother.
He was her lover and support
but her friends will hold the fort.
Single, she can mingle with kin.
Alone, his loneliness does him in.
She may confide in a sister or chum;
he may turn to a gun, gin or rum.

-9-

Old widows are sexually eschewed.
Old widowers avidly pursued.
Divorced, he can find a new mate
but she can't even get a date.
To the end, he mostly lives with his spouse;
she in nursing home or empty house.

In his final illness, she is there.
She is unpartnered in her despair.

-10-
Genders vary in biology and piety
and are patterned by society
playing out when young and old
what they were told and sold.
He and she in their old ages
can stay in conventional cages
or she can take off the mask
of dainty decorum and rasp.

-11-
Quite often in old age
women assert, seize front stage.
Earlier, not allowed to be nurturing,
men garden and are grandkids' king.
Role crossovers can take place
when men leave work's rat race
and women shed domestic roles
both fulfilling suppressed goals.

-12-
We who help people age with success
at times when they are under stress
need to know these variations.
What our old age will be
depends on whether we are he or she.

Maybe I have shocked you with that frank piece. But I could back it up by references to the scientific literature.

Indeed, I must admit that some readers were shocked by the first edition of the book. A few complained about chapter three, "Real Life Outrageousness." They questioned whether my suggestions for crashing pools and enjoying freebies might reinforce the stereotype that older women are greedy and grasping. There is some danger in this, I admit.

They also felt it was not ethical to swim when not official and certainly not dignified to be so rambunctious.

I think, however, dignity, decorum and the don'ts have limited the fun and growth of older women and that feisty is better than fright that folks will think ill of us. There is so much ageist, sexist predjudice against older women that we might as well enjoy life without worrying about others' opinions of us. They may, in fact, respect us more if we feel entitled than if we feel worthless and hide out.

I also comfort myself with the good consequences of what I do that is not exactly by the rules. When I swim in hotel pools that few use, I serve a function by stirring up the stagnant waters, for example. When I load up with free samples, I provide employment for people who make them. When I take seasoned citizens' discounts, I have some redress for all the years I worked in the workforce for lower wages than men.

I think the underdog has the right to bark. But then, I always identify with expendables. In fact, when President Clinton left Chelsea's frog in the river in Little Rock, my daughter Edith and I wrote a piece of froggerel which started:

I could have been first frog
But Clinton dumped me in a bog.

Despite my fears, readers, including good doctors, have applauded my portrayal of bad doctors in the chapter on choosing helpers. And readers have asked mental health questions. Here is an acrostic which appeared in a 1992 issue (Volume XI, no. 3) of *Hot Flash*, mentioned earlier in this book.

Aging Mental Health

A   ctivities that satisfy
G   rowth continues
I   ncome adequate
N   o undue stress
G   ood nutrition

M eaningful interactions
E mergency supports
N ew friendships
T ransportation available
A good physical check up
L ots of mental stimulation

H elping others
E xercise faithfully
A sk for help when needed
L et go of clutter
T ake time for self
H ave a religious community

It has been gratifying that many psychiatrists, social workers, psychologists and other counselors have read this book and urged their patients and clients to read it. I encourage women who need help to get it from therapists who respect clients' hard won experience and years. In fact, when teaching therapists in Continuing Education courses in hospitals and schools (Massachusetts School of Professional Psychology, Regis College, the Boston University School of Social Work, and Springfield College, School of Human Services in Manchester, New Hampshire) about older women, I usually begin by reading this poem written in the voice of a client.

Older Woman's Advice to a Therapist

What I need from you
    is support for my strengths
      rather than reminders of my flaws
      and the reinforcement of them.

What I crave from you
    is unconditional caring
      which is available nowhere else
      and never has been for me.

What I expect from you
is that my pain and terror
will not make you turn away
or offer unwanted palliatives.

What I want is that you recognize
I have surmounted huge obstacles
and have reservoirs of strength
even when hidden below despair.

What I desire is your wisdom
a place to cry for lost dreams
gathering strength to go on
imperfectly in an imperfect world.

I am constantly reminded of the ingenuity and adaptability of seasoned women. A notable example is the distinguished American novelist, Dorothy James Roberts (1903-1990) who, in the last decades of her life, was physically disabled and largely housebound. In her home, she began three activities that brought her mental stimulation and contact with people and provided a generous service. She ran a free writers' workshop to aid many women in the Palo Alto area. She taught English to Japanese and other foreign students at Stamford University and helped them with their problems. She also helped found the Colloquium where women wrote and shared scholarly papers on a wide variety of topics.

In addition, she completed extensive research on Shakespeare's plays, world mythology, and Roman history, producing and leaving behind her manuscripts of value to people in these areas. Every day, she worked at these endeavors until her death at eighty-seven.

During her long and fruitful retirement, she home-shared with Elizabeth Paschal, another remarkable elder, who is still active at age ninety-one. Besides continuing her own studies in science and mathematics, Elizabeth is supporting a project to make Dorothy's work available to students, historians, and literary scholars. (This project, under my direction, is ongoing at the Wellesley College Center for Research on Women.)

A few readers have said that I neglected one important area in the first edition. How can we survive well if we become so frail that we need institutional care?

I thought carefully about this when asked to speak at the opening of a new non-profit nursing home in Natick, MA, The Mary Ann Morse Nursing Home, part of the Metro West Hospital Campus. This prayer is the result.

My Prayer for Mary Ann Morse Nursing Home

Dear God, if possible spare me from
long illness, frailty and dependence.
But if I need to be taken care of
let me not be a burden to my children.
Help me choose good professionals
or aid my children or professionals
in choosing good caretakers for me
who are skilled and compassionate.

If I spend time in a nursing home
help me mourn my losses as I must
then enjoy what there is to enjoy,
making new friends in that setting
being a friend to others there.

Let me deepen my spirituality
thanking you for my strong years
being thankful for help in weakness.
Let me laugh as long as possible
and celebrate my life and you.

Last week, I visited two women in the same nursing home. One, confined to a wheelchair, was very cheerful and obviously much loved by the staff and residents. Although physically limited, she took part in activities at the home, talked with people, and welcomed visitors happily. She shared with me her opinion of current events. She keeps abreast by watching television and reading newspapers. I asked her about her physical condition, and she replied briefly. When a demented resident made an inappropriate remark, she smiled at the resident and shrugged at me, shrugging it off. I enjoyed the visit and will visit often. I want to spend time with this wonderful woman.

The other woman, less disabled than the first, greeted me by telling me how bored and lonely she is, how hard it is to share space. She spent the entire hour I was with her complaining in great detail about her physical problems and the neglect by her friends. She made me feel guilty that I do not visit her as often as she would like. This woman does not participate in available activities.

It is hard to be institutionalized. I hope it will not happen to me or to you. But there are ways to maximize what is available to us. Of course, it is essential to be in as good a facility as possible. Healthy older women should work to improve nursing home standards and to visit and advocate for the residents. As readers have pointed out, too often the frailest older women are ignored.

I admit this book was written especially for the well, or pretty well, older women. But we need to support our frail sisters who cannot advocate for themselves. Angry older women patients need social workers, volunteers and visitors to hear their complaints and frustrations even if listening is hard.

I will continue to visit the complainer.

*Old Women's Chant**

My time belongs to me.
I have shed responsibilities,
can choose what I do.

Knowledgeable and wise
freed from others' expectations
finally I have mastered "No."

I know who I am
a crafted, independent identity.
I like myself.

More experienced, braver,
without penalty, I speak truth.
Age licenses freedom.

I travel more,
savor women's extra seven years
creative, spiritual time.

I celebrate the power.
Millions of long-living women
scheme to change the world.

*With thanks to my graduate students in gerontology at the school of Human Services of Springfield College, Manchester, N.H.

I have learned much from my correspondents about their personal lives, but few have written about political action. We who have energy and resources need to be politically active. Women now outnumber men as voters, and we older women can get out and vote and urge others to do so. But we can do more.

I would like to relate one political action I took after writing *Be An Outrageous Older Women*. At the time of the Persian Gulf War, I became depressed because we mega-killed or wounded 200,000 human beings. Many Americans acted as if it were a victory. As you have learned, mad turned inward is sad. I was very angry at President Bush and other political leaders who could envision no action short of mass bombing and another horrible war. So I put classified ads in two magazines, *Poet* and *Poets and Writers*, asking people to send me pro-peace and anti-war poems. I received three thousand pieces of mail, many containing multiple poems. (Just ask my mailperson!)

I spent six months of my life reading and categorizing these poems about many wars, written by people in all walks of life and of all ages. The result is a powerful book containing three hundred of the most moving, diverse poems. *We Speak for Peace* was published in time for Mother's Day, May 1993 by KIT, Inc., the publisher of this *Outrageous* book.

I have been presenting readings from the *Peace* book. I hope you will read it and work for peace.

I hope you are also working for your political concerns. That will empower you and keep you vital. Collectively, it can improve our world.

It thrills me that I have inspired outrageous older women who are dangerous to bad social arrangements. Please use your crone's wisdom and power. Some women, however, have so internalized sexism and ageism that they do not know their capabilities.

When I was pondering what to write in my first "Outrageously Yours" column, I remembered a call for anonymous written questions in a workshop that yielded this one.

"I have more clothes and household possessions than I could possibly use, and I don't know what to do with my time now that I can't really go shopping anymore because I have so much stuff. I don't know what to do with myself."

Frankly, my first reaction to that question was, "What a trivial problem in view of all the major problems older women have." But then as I reflected, I realized my first thought was rather harsh and began to think what this woman's life must be like.

A wave of empathy and sympathy came over me as I realized that she was a woman who had been socialized in another era to feel that her most important function in life was to attend to her appearance and her home. Like many women of past generations, she may have received a limited education and had limited horizons. Perhaps her husband or children were not supportive of any other activities. Perhaps she had low self-esteem and was afraid to venture into new roles now that she was retired from mothering or from paid work. Perhaps she was a depressed person who used shopping and acquisition as distraction.

So, I answered her this way.

"Many people shop to fill time because they do not know about all the wonderful ways available to them. These include getting a part time job, doing volunteer work, taking courses (which are often free after sixty), enjoying Elderhostel trips and other kinds of cheap travel. For example, you can join American Youth Hostels for $15 if you are over fifty-four and stay at wonderful places with kitchens and companionship for as little as ten dollars a night. I have traveled extensively for very little money using them. (773 15th St., NW, Suite 840, Washington, D.C. 20005.)

"If you need help in figuring out how to have fun and be creative in your later years, you could join — or start — an Older Women Surviving and Thriving Group in your community. You can get the leaders' manual I have written for such groups with instructions and handouts from Families International, Inc., 11700 W. Lake Park Drive, Milwaukee, WI, 53224.

"However, if you are running to shop because you are depressed, you might need to see a therapist or physician. Sometimes, medical conditions cause depression. Sometimes, we need help in changing our life situation. Lonely people often run to stores to get away from being alone. The *Outrageous* book will teach you how to make friends.

"As an older woman, you have wisdom and experience and talents that you can use for activities other than shopping. Yet, if you have a real love and talent for shopping, perhaps you could shop for others as a volunteer or as a paid person. Many ill or frail people cannot shop for themselves or cannot drive. You could have satisfaction or profit by shopping for them. Place an ad in your local paper or work through the Council on Aging and the social agencies in your town. If you can afford to, you could also ask a shelter for battered women or an institution for children what their needs are and shop for gifts for them. You might want to become a Foster Grandparent and give to a needy child.

"Since you are so overloaded with stuff, you might give some of it to families or organizations. Sell some of your surplus clothing at a consignment shop if you need the money — then go shopping for some new styles. Or, you could give the things you don't need to Goodwill, the Salvation Army or other organizations to sell in their thrift shops which support charitable activities. Perhaps you could run a rummage sale for your religious congregation. The more you give away, the less you have to take care of, and the more time you will have for new kinds of activities.

"Instead of collecting material things, you might think of collecting your memories by writing your life story. Perhaps you could join a writing program in your community — or start one. You might also think about the things you wanted to do earlier in life for which there was not time. What new interests or hobbies could you pursue? Could you join some new organizations or become politically active, collecting signatures instead of clothes? Have a tag sale of your unneeded possessions and support women running for office with your profits.

"Read your local newspaper to see which groups are meeting and attend some of them. You might be surprised at the possibilities that open up to you. If you really love stores, could you volunteer in a food pantry that gives things away to the needy? Or could you get a part-time job in a regular store? Could you volunteer in a charitable thrift shop — or start one in your community?

"Best wishes in your quest to fill your time well."

In the workshop, I also responded to the shopper's question by reading this doggerel on volunteering.

Volunteers

The dictionary says
 a volunteer offers services
exercising free choice
for some undertaking or purpose
without obligation to do so
without payment.

I amend this to say
volunteers do get pay
for volunteering is a way
more meaningful than play
to spend an hour or day.

Volunteers have looked outward
and seen that life is hard
for some and marred
by tragedy and jarred
by crises and society's discard.
A volunteer has a good heart
and is very smart
whether pushing a bookcart
serving fruit and a tart
or addressing a part
of a problem to help start
the healing art.

You are human beings who
respond to troubles' cue
volunteering to do
work of love so true
kind through and through
and I today salute you.

During the time when I was working on this post graduate chapter, an insight came to me while I was dressing. As my insights often do, it came to me as a poem. It speaks to my situation, a women nearing seventy, and perhaps to yours.

I will never wear out my clothes
which I spent so much time finding
and nobody will want them
or the beloved paintings
collected on my travels.

It is time to cease accumulation
waste no day on the mere daily
reminisce, savor, love and laugh
leave a legacy of forgiveness
seek spirit, beauty, peace.

Today may be the last time
I pack to drive to the ocean.

The realization of our own mortality may be sudden, frightening and enraging or that realization may give us the wisdom for a good preparation for our last journey. In the last year, I have experienced many relationship losses, part of late life.

Grace, Megan, Sophie, Margaret, Nat

How dared you all die this year.
This year, when I, near seventy
need your strength and friendship.

And Lisa, how can you be frail
immobilized when I want laughter
and a good companion for adventure?

Mary, you go to sleep at seven
and don't dress until eleven
your sparkle flat as bedsheets.

It is simply not appropriate
that we growing old bury the old
bring soup and solace to the sick.

Were I in charge of arrangements
you would dance at my 90th birthday
bearing champagne, flowers, jokes.

It was therapeutic for me to write that poem.

If you recall, I also urged the shopper to write. Actually, I urge all women to write, especially their memoirs. We have so much knowledge and experience that has been left out of books. I took my own advice and, for the first semester of 1992-93, went to Mount Holyoke College in beautiful South Hadley, MA to be a resident at the Five Colleges Women's Studies Research Center sponsored by Mount Holyoke, Smith College, Amherst College, Hampshire College and the University of Massachusetts. There, I wrote the first draft of *my* memoir and am now revising it. It was a wonderful way to work. One of the most valuable parts of the experience was being with marvelous women from all over and making new friends.

We women need to make new friends throughout life and such friendships require reciprocity. This truth is stated metaphorically in a poem I put under the door of the office across the hall occupied by Charlotte Templin, a professor of English from Indianapolis University. (The poem has been published in *Hemetera*, the literary magazine of Regis college.)

Fall Harvest

Charlotte, three times
we have exchanged pears.
In return for my apple,
you presented me with
a sturdy green pear
which ripened perfectly.

Then I gave you a Bartlett
splotched brown by the sun.
Today you presented me
with a yellow and red
aristocratic pear
to enjoy aesthetically.

I look at this beauty
ripening like friendship.

While at the Five Colleges Women Studies Center, I also resonated
to a web sculpture in the apple orchard below my study window.

Letter to a Feminist Sculptor

Dear Cristina Biaggi
I thought you should know
spiders have discovered
your web here at Mount Holyoke.
They have spun silk strands
delicate silver among your
strong ropes chrysanthemum
pink, purple, red, orange.

A squirrel has taken the web
for her special playground.
The apples play ball aiming
through the web's holes

to nurture waiting insects
in the soft grass below.
The migrating birds fly by
singing wonder and joy.

I visit your web daily.
Cristina, here is my strand
here is my play and my song.
I am in the web and under it
the web encloses, embraces.
The hanging globes comfort me.
They are whole, strong.
They make me whole, strong.

The web is tied securely.
The earth is still strong.
Women are growing stronger
The earth will survive.
I will survive too.
I was at Seneca Falls
I was at the Pentagon.
I was connected then.

Near seventy, I still
work for world peace
My book, *We Speak for Peace*,
is my web made of pacifists
but sometimes I am discouraged
at all the violence and war.
Your web gives me courage.
Thank you Cristina Biaggi.

At the Five Colleges Center I also was captivated by a portrait in
the seminar room and describe it below.

Found Portrait — Found Poem

The unknown woman's portrait
was rescued from under a couch
in the dead furniture storage
At Mount Holyoke College
by Gail Hornstein
and hung in the seminar room
of the Five Colleges
Women's Studies Research Center

A 19th century beauty
well dressed, winged hat
seemingly self assured
Was this woman real
or an artist's vision?
Was the artist a man
or woman, young or old?
Was it a self portrait
of who she was
or who she desired to be?
Was she a professor
a student, dean, donor?

Was she a wife and mother
cherished or abused
was the beauty dimmed
by yearly pregnancies
or being devalued
when she aged.
Was she unmarried
living on her father's funds
or a pioneer in a profession?

Was she a lover of women
was she a friend to women

did she die young or live
to be a beautiful old woman.

Was she like us
a strong woman coping
in a world run by men?

I have also established new friendships with readers of the *Outrageous* book. One, Nancy Welch of Center Harbor, New Hampshire was kind enough to write to ENCORE saying, "I have joined the ranks of the outrageous and have found that Dr. Ruth has given me tremendous courage and strength."

I have also thankfully deepened my friendships with Sandra Brown and Rita McCullough, KIT co-publishers.

Advocacy by Older Women

A   dvocacy by older American women reviewed.

D   id Maggie Kuhn accept involuntary retirement?

V   iolated by this, she and six friends started the Grey Panthers.

O   r did Tish Somers swallow discrimination for older widows and divorcees?

C   alifornia legislators heard her and passed displaced homemaker aid.

A   nd Laurie Shields joined and continued in this D.H. work.

C   ould Jane Porcino find a new way to advocate for older women?

Y   es, she started NAFOW and its great newsletter, *Hot Flash*.

B   ut also many less known fed up older women

Y   elled at legislators, picketed, wrote letters.

O   lder women in many states competently and vigorously

L   ead Older Women's League Chapters, supporting President Lou Glasse,

D   evoting themselves to economic issues of older women.

E   ven the American Association of Retired Persons

R   ecently started a Women's Initiative with elder spokespersons.

A t professional meetings and other organizations
M arvelous feisty old women make sure that committees and
E lections include old women ending their invisibility.
R etired women are actively pursuing political issues
I n urban, rural, suburban communities throughout America.
C apable older women serve as nursing home ombudspersons
A nd make waves about elder neglect, abuse and exploitation.
N ow a new breed of strong matriarchs and prophets

W ill assert for their rights and a better society
O utrageously celebrating their aging wisdom.
M eekness and silence is eschewed finally.
E nergy abounds from post menopausal zest.
N ew breeds of croned advocates laugh and thrive.

And remember this alphabet.

An Alphabet for Aging Well

A is for ACTIVITY
better than passivity
B is for BRAVERY
with some comic knavery
C is for CARING
D is for DARING
E is for ERRING
F is for FORGIVING others and yourself and
FREELY living

G is for GIVING but also GETTING
H is for HEALING
I is for INSPIRATION

J is for JOKES and fun
K for KNOWLEDGE,
of which we have a ton
L is for LOVE in old age

M is for MATRIARCHS, very sage.
N is for NATURE profound and for beauty to enjoy all around.

O is for OPPORTUNITY
to attend the university
in our later years
with young people and age peers.
P is for wise PATRIARCHS
old men who get good marks.
Q is for QUESTS and QUESTIONING
that makes our brains sing.
R is for REMINISCENCE
remembering our lives' dance.
S is for SEXUALITY
which is not banality.
T is for THEATER and TRAVEL
and truths still to unravel.

U is for UNDERSTANDING
long life has given us.
V is for variety and VITALITY.
W is for our WISE WORDS
X is for XEROXING
to send those words
like birds flying.

Y is for YOU, survivor seers,
greeting your later years
with Z for ZEST
with cheers, not tears
or fears, my dears.
Our alphabet is done.
Your challenge has begun.

Older women already have courage and strength to have survived in a difficult society. But I hope my words have reinforced these qualities.

Be outrageous and courageous. Respect yourself. Give and get. Groan if oppressed, but grow.

> Older women will hack new roles
> with a teaspoon out of permafrost.
> When you compliment their strength,
> they will offer you a spoonful.
> They will build welcoming homes
> from Scotch tape and garage sales.
> When you sink into the comfort,
> they will say "anyone could do it."
> They will share their lifesaving wisdom
> sending no bill for their services
> and thank you for listening.
>
> Thank you for listening to me.